THE ETHICS OF UNCERTAINTY

RELATED TITLES PUBLISHED BY ONEWORLD

What Christians Believe, David Craig, ISBN 1–85168–218–X
Jesus: A Short Biography, Martin Forward, ISBN 1–85168–172–8
The Fifth Dimension, John Hick, ISBN 1–85168–191–4
A Concise Encyclopedia of Christianity, Geoffrey Parrinder, ISBN 1–85168–174–4
Christianity: A Short Introduction, Keith Ward, ISBN 1–85168–229–5
God, Faith and the New Millennium, Keith Ward, ISBN 1–85168–155–8

THE ETHICS OF UNCERTAINTY

A New Christian Approach to
Moral Decision-Making

R. John Elford

ONEWORLD

OXFORD

For my children Emily and Robert

THE ETHICS OF UNCERTAINTY

Oneworld Publications
(Sales and Editorial)
185 Banbury Road
Oxford OX2 7AR
England
http://www.oneworld-publications.com

Oneworld Publications
(US Marketing Office)
160 N Washington St.
4th Floor, Boston
MA 02114
USA

ISBN 1–85168–217–1

Library of Congress Cataloging-in-Publication Data

Cover design by Design Deluxe
Typeset by Saxon Graphics, Derby, UK
Printed and bound by Clays Ltd, St Ives plc

CONTENTS

ACKNOWLEDGEMENTS

The dedication of this book to my teenage children Emily and Robert is out of gratitude for their tolerating, over the years, a father whose absences from home to write have been on top of those also required by a busy ministerial and academic life. It also reflects my awareness that making continued progress in the many issues here discussed will be increasingly up to their generation.

Without the support of many colleagues at Liverpool Hope University College this book could not have been written. My senior colleague, Professor Simon Lee, kindly agreed to partial secondment from other duties and has done so much to encourage the development of the teaching and researching of theology in the College in central fulfilment of its Mission. Professor Ian Markham helped to plan the book and support its writing. In a timely way, he also invited me to give the Hope Theology Lectures on the subject in the autumn of 1998. Dr Kenneth Newport, Dr Tinu Ruparell and Dr J'annine Jobling have read passages relating to their specialisms and been willing to engage in innumerable discussions. Mr Alfred Westwell has obligingly copy-edited and corrected drafts and Mr Christopher Williams has regularly provided research and other practical support. I am sincerely grateful to them all for their professional willingness, good company and friendship. Any shortcomings in what follows are, of course, entirely my own responsibility.

John Elford
Liverpool Hope University College

INTRODUCTION

Human beings, as far as we know, are unique in their ability to choose right from wrong. Their endeavour to do this correctly is as old as their civilisation and coterminous with its religious, philosophical and literary history. Not all religions treat morality in the same way, largely as a consequence of their social settings. Likewise, philosophies vary in the extent to which they give prominence to ethical over other concerns. The theme of ethics is, however, interwoven between them. As religions and philosophies have changed over the centuries, so too have the ways they have treated morality, with the result that understandings of ethics are so much a part of the spirit of their life and times that they often provide a unique window into it. For these and other reasons, understandings of morality have always been, and still are, changing as they exist alongside each other both competitively and interactively. In chapter 1 we will explore precisely what is meant by the term 'ethics', but for now we need only reflect on these more general considerations about its place in ever unfolding human history.

Another word, 'morality', is often used in conjunction with 'ethics' and this, alone, often causes confusion. 'Ethics', like 'physics', is one of those rare singular words in English which ends with an 's', a reason for yet more common confusion. Some writers have used 'ethics' to refer to the question of individual moral conduct and 'morality' to refer to the question of collective moral conduct. There is, as we shall see, an important distinction to be made between individual and collective morality, but no clear purpose can be served by designating these two terms to each of them exclusively. The two words are best treated as

1

synonyms. The use of one or the other in what follows is invariably dictated by nothing more than stylistic preference.

This book is about a particular challenge presented to ethics in our own life and times and the way in which it can be particularly well met by the Christian moral tradition as it has come to be reinterpreted in recent years. That challenge is the challenge of 'uncertainty' and, again, we will consider in detail what the word means in this context. Broadly, it draws attention to the fact that when we make moral decisions we are invariably both methodologically unsure and often overwhelmed by the sheer complexity of the factors which need to be taken into account, with the result that we are left more in hope than in certainty that we have ever done the right thing. The desire to avoid this often unpleasant experience, not unnaturally, gives rise to attempts to find certainty in morality, if for no other reason than to enjoy the peace of mind that this affords. Throughout what follows we will consider critically some of the ways in which such certainty is now sought, particularly in the Christian tradition. In this it will become clear that there is, in fact, no refuge to be found in certainty alone and that, as a result, the implications of living with uncertainty cannot, and more to the point need not, be avoided.

Uncertainty, as we shall again see, is arguably a feature of our worldwide cultural circumstances as we enter the third millennium. Its effects are all-embracing as they permeate the lives of people everywhere. There may still be a few primitive cultures in which life has not changed over the centuries and where we find them we should treat them with the greatest of respect, but for the vast majority such primitive stability has long since ceased to be a realistic option. Some, of course, try to preserve it amid the change of all else, but they, again, are few. Modernity, then, and uncertainty are seemingly inseparable and if we want the benefits of the former, which most of us for good reason do, then we cannot escape the difficulties of the latter. We will explore some of the many reasons why uncertainty is arguably the leitmotif of our age and why, also, we will thrive best when we come to terms with that and discover what to do about it. In many ways, it is caused by the simple fact that we live in an age of widespread moral disagreement. This alone is sufficient to cause uncertainty in the minds of any but those who find refuge in bigotry. Constant debate and disagreement of this kind causes its participants and onlookers alike to ask whether the real answers will ever be found. Such debate engenders diminishing confidence in once seemingly well established systems of morality, particularly those which claimed that the truths of morality were self-evident and required only that we do our duty by conforming to them. Most important of all is the uncertainty caused by the increasingly evident limitations of our knowledge.

Because uncertainty is as widespread as it is, all religions, philosophies and systems of morality now have to address its implications for what they believe if they are to maintain their credibility – once, that is, the luxury of taking refuge in false certainties has been rejected. Along with such rejections of certainty, as we shall again see, the view that there has ever been or can be a system of morality which is unchanging and impervious to what is happening around and about it has to go. This then presents other problems, particularly in religious moralities because they are so often bound up with systems of authority which appear, at least, to be certain and unchanging. We will explore the need for an alternative basis for authority in morality, one based not on certainty, but on the integrity with which it comes to terms, not only with what we know, but more importantly with what we do not. Such authority will be seen to be contextual rather than objective. It will derive its strength from its own life blood in given situations and not from some 'other' source alone. The tensions which understanding authority in this way can create, (and we will consider some of them), are for some unbearable because they require the *creation* of value rather than, simply, its slavish application.

None of this, as we shall see, is to suggest that we must live in the present alone with no recourse to the wisdom of the ages to come to our aid. Far from it. 'Presentism', as it may be termed, is little short of an unacceptable arrogance. Human beings have always wrestled with their moral dilemmas and it behoves us to study why, how and with what success our predecessors have done so, not because we can opt out of our own dilemmas by copying them, but because we will be able to cope better with ours if we steep ourselves in the knowledge of how they coped with theirs. One reason for this is that, though times and circumstances may change radically, human beings change but little in comparison. Matters of the heart remain much the same as they ever have been and will be: of love and hatred, of insecurity and the desire for the welfare of offspring. All this is why poetry and art speak across the ages as, for example, when we read great literature like the Book of Job and see it for the profound essay on the human condition that it is and will ever remain. Coming to terms with the present, therefore, does not at all require that we ignore the past. Quite the reverse, we ignore it at our peril.

This combination of listening to the past yet recognising a framework of uncertainty will, to some, seem very post-modern. However this is not the case. As we shall see, my view of history is broadly modernist and the uncertainty framework Kantian. Suffice it to say that I take the view that 'post-modernism' is an ill-defined and pluriform concept, beyond the fact that all its many uses seem to have in common a dismissal of modernism whatever, again, that might have been or be. We will discuss this further in chapter 2. This dismissal of modernity is often so strident that what is postmodern is thought to be, by definition, whatever is anti-modern. Whilst there is much of value in this debate, we will not engage with it extensively even though others might judge what follows according to its tenets. We will see why the past remains ever relevant to the present, however different from the present it may seem to be. We will also see why awareness of the past need not require an unquestioning deference to it which debilitates our ability to face the future. All previous futures, just like our own, have contained uncertainty and we would be guilty of the arrogance of presentism if we thought otherwise. All that is being claimed here is that uncertainty is now all-pervading and most evident where we most need it not to be when we seek to make the right moral decisions. We will also note, however, why it is that uncertainty also plays an important role in both individual and corporate endeavour.

In the later chapters of this book we will explore theoretically and by way of practical examples, what it means to say and live with the fact that even the best of our moral endeavours will remain provisional ones: will remain, that is, continually subject to review and revision in the light of new knowledge and needs. So understood, the moral life becomes an exciting part of the general flux of human life, rather than something which stands over and against it. There is, of course, nothing particularly new in suggesting that even the best of our moral endeavours have to remain provisional ones. Aristotle, in a more limited way, pointed this out long ago when he claimed that ethics was a branch of politics because it is the responsibility of the state to create conditions in which citizens can enjoy the opportunity of living the good life. With all this done, however, he reminds us that: 'It is the mark of the educated man and a proof of his culture that in every subject he looks only for so much precision as its nature permits.'[1] In precisely this spirit we will see why, contrary to what is often thought about Christian morality, it is particularly able to meet widespread uncertainty and the provisionality in morality uncertainty engenders and even demands. This will become clear, not by inventing some new understanding of Christianity, but rather by drawing on some of its orthodoxies and seeing them for the radical ideas they often are when they are applied to our needs in general and to our moral ones in particular.

Central to these orthodoxies will be those of the biblical traditions and we will need to refer to them throughout. These will be seen to be dynamic rather than static and those who believe they are the reverse will be shown to be seriously misrepresenting them. The Bible, remember, contains writings which span at least a millennium and the earliest of these reach back into centuries of preceding oral traditions. As would be expected, this vast time-span embraces many different cultures and outlooks. Attempts to homogenise these into 'the biblical view of x' will be seen to be false. Modern biblical scholarship has, generally, enabled us to understand the rich diversity of views on all manner of things in the biblical traditions by showing how they were seldom, if ever, either static or coherent. This is particularly the case with the biblical writings on morality, not least because they, in turn, are an inseparable part of wider historical and theological developments. We will see not only how the biblical faith was always 'in the making' throughout biblical times, but also, and importantly, how it must remain so if it is to continue to call itself biblical. We will contrast the acceptability of this view with the widespread but mistaken notion that what the Bible really requires is static conformity to its diktats.

We will also see how at least two other Christian orthodoxies are important. The first is drawn from Christian eschatology, its understanding of the 'last things'. This stresses that in the future Kingdom of God all values and love will be revealed, but that this side of that Kingdom our knowledge is imperfect and partial. St Paul put this memorably when he claimed that: 'For now we see in a mirror dimly, but then we shall see face to face. Now I know only in part; then I will know fully, even as I have been fully known.' (1 Cor. 13: 12.) Christian eschatology in this way seeks to understand the relationship of the last to present things. In the Pauline and other biblical traditions it does this by believing that what we know now is a glimpse, albeit an imperfect and provisional one, of a greater reality. The appropriateness of eschatology of this kind to an understanding of morality which has to come to terms with uncertainty generated by the incompleteness of our knowledge will be recognised. The second element of Christian doctrine which will be shown to be important is that which claims that human life is most fulfilled when it is upheld by the sustaining grace of a loving God. So understood, grace is the means whereby God communicates God's self to God's creatures. This was supremely, but not exclusively, achieved in the life of Jesus. Grace, so understood, is an activity, a part of the moral and spiritual life. The manner of its precise operation has been and still is the subject of ongoing debate in the Christian tradition. We will discuss this and show its relevance to morality.

All this will be a wider contribution to an ongoing reinterpretation of Christian morality which has begun to take place in recent years. For the most part, this has focused on the New Testament and, in particular, on the place of morality in the teaching of Jesus. An important contribution to this new debate was made by Nicholas Peter Harvey in *The Morals of Jesus,* which appeared in 1991.[2] He makes two central observations: 'that there is an endemic human craving for a moral system, [and] … that many people tend to project onto Jesus as the validating exemplar of such a system'.[3] The result is the existence of a widespread distortion of what Jesus said about morality. In order to find out what that actually was, Harvey re-examines the, so-called, 'hard sayings' of Jesus about morality. These are the many sayings recorded throughout the gospels which seem to contradict what are commonly believed to be the requirements of Christian morality. As a result of this re-examination, he concludes that Jesus was 'characteristically unconcerned with ethics in any of the usual meanings of the word'.[4] Meanings, that is, which are usually translated into 'should' and 'should not'. What emerges from this study is a picture of Jesus which serves as a guide to the moral life but in a more generally disturbing than reassuring way. Christian morality, Harvey argues, must focus on the death of Jesus as the illustration of the limit of human achievement. Only in this way can the freedom of the Christian life be appropriated. When this is experienced it becomes possible for us to explore new and creative dimensions of Christian morality and, in doing so, discover what being fully human means in a Christian sense. In this brief book Harvey does not explore his claims in any detail nor does he discuss their wider significance for contemporary Christian morality and its cultural setting, but he makes two extremely important points. The first is that the place of morality in the teaching of Jesus is almost universally misunderstood and the second is that a more accurate understanding of that morality is far more liberating for the human spirit. After we have also re-examined the place of morality in the teaching of Jesus and in the biblical tradition more generally, with reference to recent biblical scholarship, by way of illustration we will consider the wider implications of this sort of reinterpretation of Christian morality in chapter 6. In the final chapter we will suggest one way of understanding how the liberation of the human spirit takes place in Christian morality, through the operation of divine grace.

Even at this point, it may seem strange to some that the orthodoxy of Christian love has not, thus far at least, been mentioned. Is not this, they might ask, *the* central orthodoxy of Christian morality? We will see that it *is* central, but not for the reasons that are commonly supposed. Some suggest that love is so central that, in any situation of moral choice, all that is required of us is that we do the loving thing and that this alone will suffice.[5] Much reference to the Bible is often quoted in support of this. But such reference is selective in the extreme. Contrary to popular belief, love is never the sole determining factor. St Paul, for example, always links it to other factors such as becoming Christ-like, and other New Testament writers are far from in agreement with each other when they write on the topic. Even in the Bible itself, then, there is no clear agreement that love alone is always a guide to action. We will see why it most certainly should not be considered so. Sincere disagreements about what love requires are common in moral debate among Christians and they will ever remain so this side of the Kingdom of God. Notwithstanding this serious shortcoming, love remains important for two reasons. First, it is what can inspire us to moral action, what motivates us to want to do something in the first place. This, of course, is no small thing in itself. Even more than this, love is what can sustain us in our moral endeavours and never more so than when they seem fruitless. All this is the stuff of often heroic self-sacrifice and, for that reason, it can be moving in the extreme. 'No one has greater love than this, to lay down one's life for one's friends.' (John 15: 13.) Love, in this way, remains central to the Christian moral life.

Chapter One

A MODERN ETHICAL DILEMMA

Every age has had to face its own distinctive ethical dilemmas which have arisen largely from the movements of human history. This book is about one single feature which affects human beings at the beginning of the third millennium CE. It is not new, but it is different because of the urgency with which it presses itself. That feature, as we have seen, is the feature of *uncertainty,* and it affects human life in all manner of ways. We will discuss just one of these; the effect of uncertainty on our understanding of morality in general and Christian morality in particular. To begin with, we need to have some definition of what is meant by the word 'morality', since it is a notoriously slippery concept.

Ethics, at least for those of us living in the Western philosophical tradition, manifests itself in three related principal ways: the human, the factual and the philosophical–religious. When we have considered these we will add a fourth: the subject of this book, uncertainty.

Human beings are unique in their ability to make ethical choices because they can reason about the options available to them and because they also have the freedom and the will which enables them to implement those choices. When they do this well they prosper and when they do it badly they frequently suffer from the consequences of doing so. The most poignant example of the latter is the experience of tragedy, in a classical sense, which can result from wrong choice. It exemplifies the fact that things could have been other than they tragically are, if other choices had been made. Tragedy, then, is compounded with human responsibility and culpability. Literature, from the Greek tragedians to the present time, is redolent with essays on this aspect of the human condition which, for whatever reason, never ceases to fascinate. Perhaps this is because, in tragic circumstances of our own making, we become starkly aware of the promethean dimension of our powers, in the sense that we can be overwhelmed by them, as well as of the fact that things could have been other than as they tragically are if we had chosen other than as we did. Little wonder that discussions about ethics of this kind plumb the depths of what it means to be human. Happily for the human lot, the majority of our moral choices occur in more everyday and manageable circumstances, difficult though they often remain.

The human manifestation of ethics is, then, inescapable and profoundly personal in the sense that it affects every single human individual. We might wish that things were otherwise, but the fact is that none of us can escape the central obligation of making ethical choices. Going along with others or taking the lines of least resistance are the ways in which most of us cope with this for most of the time, but even here we bear responsibility for our actions. The desire to conform, however, is a strong one and itself explains why morality is so vulnerable to swings of opinion and fashion. It also explains why life can often be so difficult for those who question this. Little wonder why so much moral debate becomes emotive and passionate, often in the extreme. Indeed, some recent writers on ethics have even fastened on this aspect of it to define its very essence. Most commentators, however, now consider such an emphasis to be unacceptably reductionist in the sense that it ignores other important aspects of what it means to be moral. Suffice it to observe here that morality is intensely and unavoidably individual; a central part of the human lot. However, individual though it might initially be and largely remain, there is more to it, since ethical problems are rarely faced by any human being alone. They share with each other a knowledge of, as well as responsibility for, their moral actions. This is why the human manifestation of ethics has a collective as well as an individual face. Individual ethical preferences exist alongside and overlap with collective ones. They colour each other, but are in important respects different. These differences are subject to widespread disagreement but they are as important to our right understanding of individual and collective morality as they are to our seeing how the two fit into a wider whole. The dramas of individual life are mirrored in collectivities and, moreover, often complicated by them. Let a simple example which is common in ethical debate illustrate some of these issues.

If an individual has to contemplate the awesome decision of whether or not, given certain circumstances, it is right to take the life of another, the highest aspiration she or he might seek, and seek properly, is that of self-sacrifice. Accordingly such an individual in pursuit of this end might decide not to exercise physical self-defence which would be likely to result in and even require the death of an assailant in order to save her or his own life. Difficult though such a decision as this is, it is straightforward when compared to whether or not such an individual should contemplate taking the life of another to save that of a third party or parties. Here it will need to be asked whether the individual making the decision has the right to decide whether or not it is proper to act self-sacrificially, or whether or not that other has a reasonable right to expect, for whatever reason, that she or he will be defended. The defence of loved ones or those too young or old or frail to defend themselves is an obvious example. The self-sacrifice of the acting individual is not the prime consideration or even the highest motive here. Duty to others plays an obvious part as does, more generally, the desire to see justice done. In other words, the circumstances under which an ethical act is evaluated are different in the two cases. So different that some conclude that there are two different moralities here, the private and the public.[1] This example illustrates the difference. It all becomes much more complex when we ask questions about the rightness or wrongness of nations going to war and of how people who object to that in conscience are treated. These discussions are well known and never go away, given that the world is as it is.

Difficult ethical choices can often cause individuals to flourish or perish, and this can also be true of whole societies. The latter can become discredited and even destroyed if they pursue non-moral courses of action. The apartheid regime in South Africa is an obvious and recent illustration of this. Its central ethical values were increasingly unacceptable to the wider international community and it could not continue to exist once its repeated resort to force and constraint was challenged internally. In the face of all this the collapse of the regime became inevitable. The same is, thankfully and hopefully, now happening in Ireland, the Middle East and elsewhere as those on both sides of the divide whose resort was to terrorism are being coerced, by whatever means, to join the peace processes.

This human manifestation of ethics is, for all these and other reasons, the stuff of the drama of human life and, for that reason alone, the subject of a great deal of the world's literature. Human beings have never been able to escape these obligations and never will be able to as long as life remains as it is. But there is, of course, much more to ethical problems than this.

Another important way in which ethics manifests itself is that it always comprises factual circumstances. Actual ethical decisions, unlike theoretical ones which can exist *in vacuo,* always exist at a given time and under particular circumstances. Indeed, they are often precipitated by some change in factual circumstance. The threat of attack, to return to the earlier illustrative theme, is an obvious example. But notice the first thing about this: it is open to differing interpretations. While some might perceive such a threat to be real and imminent, others may dispute this. The dramas of the British Government in 1938 under Neville Chamberlain are etched on everyone's mind as an illustration of this. 'Peace in our time' and a small piece of paper waved above his head as he stepped off the plane after discussions with Adolf Hitler were enough for some to conclude that the Nazi threat was either an illusion or, at least, not imminent, in which case the existing process of British rearmament need not be accelerated. How different it all became even before the ink was dry. The actual circumstances required drastic action as it became clear that immediate armed resistance to the Nazi threat was for the vast majority, even some who had been long-time pacifists, the only acceptable moral response. Let another, this time contemporary, illustration make the same point. The acceptability or otherwise of genetically modified foodstuffs has suddenly become the centre of intense ethical debate. At its heart is the simple question of whether or not they are harmful to human beings and the wider food chain. We do not know the answer to this. Claims for and against are repeatedly made in what looks like a media story that is being made to run and run, but we remain largely ignorant of fundamental facts given the current state of knowledge in the subject. All this explains why we cannot decide on the finer ethical issues relating to the debate. The extent of our ignorance will be the theme of a subsequent discussion of our contemporary ethical dilemma. Here it is referred to only to make this simple point.

Another feature of the factual manifestation of ethics is, of course, that presented by the scarcity of so many of the resources which are necessary for human well-being. This is often caused by economic stringencies which prevent us from being able to provide for everyone all the things they need. Examples of this can be remarkably simple: imagine two patients, both need access to a life-support machine but only one machine is available, and all the difficulties that creates. But there are yet other major difficulties relating to the factual manifestation of ethics.

In any given instance it is often difficult to decide which facts are relevant to a particular ethical problem and which ones are not. What frequently happens is that a prior decision for or against the ethical case itself colours the interpretation of the facts under discussion. Let us take again another recent example of extreme importance.

Those who accepted the ethical correctness of nuclear deterrence theory in the 1980s, under the Thatcher Conservative Government in the UK of that period, invariably did so because they believed, like Mrs Thatcher, that the weapons so deployed, had 'kept the peace in Europe for thirty years'. She believed, that is, that there was a demonstrable causal connection between the deployment and the peace. Other observers disagreed. They saw those deployments, conversely, as the reason why the peace was unstable and becoming exponentially more so, as the need for them was used to justify the then rampant nuclear arms race. The ethical debates of the period and immediately afterwards were redolent with factual claim and counter claim. Moral philosophers have argued this issue in recent times and one of the things they have stressed is the need to distinguish between facts which are 'brute relative' in the sense of being significant to ethical problems and those which are simply 'brute' in the sense that they are not. This philosophical debate is close to another when the factual elements of ethics are being discussed. This is the Naturalistic Fallacy, so called by those who believe that it is wrong to reduce ethical discussion to factual issues. Others question whether this is a fallacy at all. The philosophical detail of these arguments need not detain us here beyond this mention, not because it is unimportant, but because it is well documented elsewhere.[2]

The third manifestation of ethics is that of the 'ethical resources' on which people draw when they make ethical decisions. We all live in ethical communities, whether we are consciously aware of them or not. All such communities have their ethical histories and traditions. Some of these are religious and some secular and some are mixtures of the two. For the most part, these ethical resources of our communities will be tacit rather than explicit and appear as custom and habit which is built up historically and handed down from one generation to the next. Preliterate communities often did this orally and we have some remarkable examples of this which were later committed to writing. One such is the so-called Wisdom Literature of the Old Testament, which is also found in Egyptian and Mesopotamian literatures. This varied literature, in part, reaches back into Israel's nomadic past when the education of the young was largely achieved by passing on to them the wisdom of the elders. All cultures do this in some way or other. Religious traditions of ethics, of course, also achieve this education through the rituals of worship. In the Christian tradition, Bible reading and study are central to this. We will discuss this later in some detail.

Secular ethical traditions are largely philosophical in origin and, for that reason, can be traced to influential philosophers and the movements generated by their work. Just like the religious traditions of ethics, these are remarkably durable in the sense that their influence spans the centuries. Ethics in Western culture is still influenced by the Socratic philosophers of the fourth and fifth centuries BCE as well as by *their* antecedents. More recent important examples of the philosophical origin of our ethical values will be discussed in what follows. So, we live out our ethical lives largely unaware of all this and only have to do otherwise when we are forced by some circumstance or other to be explicit about why we act as we do.

Whilst these manifestations of ethics often come separately into focus, at other times they overlap each other in ever-changing ways. Sometimes the interaction is between the human and the factual, at others it is the human overlapping with tradition in a dynamic and never-ceasing process. With these manifestations in mind we are frequently able to unravel something of the complexity of all this, whenever we try to understand reflectively why we act as we do. Indeed, some of the best debates about ethics occur when people of different ethical traditions communicate with each other and when they are, in turn, in discussion with technical experts of one kind or another. But none of this is simple. Quite often the traditions colour the facts and, in so doing, impede the making of any real progress. Contemporary ethical debate is bedevilled by examples of this. This is why serious enquirers into ethics often have to insist that empirical and scientific information is taken seriously however disturbing it might be to cherished views and practices. One important example of this can be found in debates about ecology, the environment and the wider created order. The World Council of Churches has long been promoting discussion about this under the slogan of 'Justice, Peace and the Integrity of Creation', with the implication that the created order has a purpose and sustainability in the observation of which we can discover something of the intentions of its Creator. In an important recent article, co-authored by a natural scientist and a theologian, this has been challenged. The scientist, Charles Birch, shows conclusively why the created order is unstable and of limited life. The theologian, Ronald Preston, points out why this requires theologians to come to terms with the often, for them, uncomfortable fact that God's providence to his creatures will eventually cease and that, in the meantime, its adequacy towards them all cannot be taken for granted.[3] Even such a simple correction of the assumed facts as this can require widespread changes of mind and policy in public opinion. When the latter is entrenched in certain quarters of institutions such as the Churches we should be under no illusion about the effort required to change perceptions if progress is to be made.

We will later see, to the credit of many of the Christian Churches, that they have been and are particularly active and painstaking in contemporary ethical debates. Some of them, moreover, display a genuine willingness to accept changes of mind and attitude on serious ethical issues and this often causes them no end of internal turmoil and difficulty. A clear example of that is seen recently in the 1998 Lambeth Conference of Anglican Bishops. That Church is willingly engaged in a debate about the nature of homosexuality and about the implications of our changing knowledge of this widespread and profound human condition. But in this it has met a radical disagreement amongst its membership and has been, at times, hard put to handle the internal debate this has caused. The recently observed triumph of a backlash against more liberal attitudes is itself causing new difficulties for the Anglican Church as it seeks to continue the debate. We will later consider in more detail this and other examples of changing Christian opinion on particular ethical issues.

As we have seen, there is now a new and invariably common feature in ethical debate across a range of issues. Unless we understand it we will scarcely be able to make progress. That feature is *uncertainty*. Time and again when we face these issues, we are confronted by an uncertainty which presents itself in innumerable ways. In the next chapter we will consider wider cultural and philosophical reasons why this is happening, for now we will consider only how it manifests itself in morality. This happens, broadly, in two ways. First, the fundamental categories on which ethics has been traditionally premised are no longer accepted as they once were without question. Second, we are now confronted by a number of identifiable phenomena with which we have to cope whenever we want to act morally. We shall now see that both of these, in their own ways, generate uncertainty.

The fundamental categories on which ethics has been widely premised, but which now generate uncertainty are: deontology, natural law, utilitarianism, and the Hidden Hand. We will now consider each of these in turn.

Deontology is, strictly, the study of duty. It proceeds from the assumption that there are ethical values which are good in themselves and which, for that reason alone, must be observed even, and this is the point, if they give rise to ethically unacceptable circumstances. This is why deontological ethics is concerned, amongst other things, with the notions of 'duty', 'obligation' and the 'intrinsic rightness' of actions. Two common examples of such are truth telling and not killing other human beings. Such ethical values, a deontologist would argue, are intrinsically virtuous in the sense that they require no further or extrinsic justification. It is, therefore, our duty to observe them, regardless of *any* indications to the contrary. The ethical agent who does this, so the theory goes, is virtuous by dint of adherence to the principle at stake and is not to be held responsible for any morally undesirable consequences which might follow. This view of ethics is obviously congenial to religious believers who think that there are divinely revealed rules, such as the Ten Commandments, which must be obeyed strictly, if our actions are to receive the divine favour. That these rules are largely negative and prohibitive in character does not matter. They stand in their own right and their authority derives solely from the dramatic nature of their origins as, for example, does the Mosaic Law. They are absolute and that is the end of the matter. This view is extremely ancient and was a common feature of ancient Near Eastern morality in general and that of Israelite religion in particular. It also features strongly in Islamic ethics and to this day among fundamentalist groups of all kinds. Numerous contemporary writers on ethics such as W.D. Ross, John Rawls and John Finnis can be described as deontologists.

By far the most influential 'modern' deontologist, however, was Immanuel Kant whose great essay, *Groundwork of the Metaphysic of Morals,* retains widespread influence.[4] This view of Kant has been challenged on the grounds that he was more concerned to take the consequences of actions into account than is widely believed, but the more traditional view of him as a deontologist prevails.[5] Kant's ethics are part of his wider views about religion. Morality, he argues, ineluctably leads to religion because the supreme good is not fully attainable in this life and immortality must, therefore, exist. Since the ethical life, so understood, is partially available in this life it behoves us to be ethical. In *Groundwork,* Kant located the essence of ethics in the freedom of the will, which alone, he argued, is good. 'It is impossible', he writes, 'to conceive anything at all in the world, or even out of it, which can be taken as good without qualification, except a *good will.*'[6] He goes on from this to claim that actions done, by the exercise of free-will, from duty have their moral worth solely as acts of duty and not as a consequence of the purposes attained by them. Similar laws can be appropriated by using the so-called 'Golden Rule'. Christianity is a good example of this: 'Do unto others as you would be done unto.' This is generally known as the 'universalisability' requirement which Kant made much of. It claims that things are intrinsically right if we will them to be universally obligatory and wrong if we do not. Again, however, there are problems with this. Perhaps individuals, such as masochists, like things done to themselves which it would clearly be improper if they did to others. There is no end to the list of things which some individuals like done to themselves which would be clearly improper if done unto others. Kant defends his view against the claim that there is a moral value in telling lies if, for example, a life can be saved as a result. The duty of truth telling, he counters, is greater than the desirability of *any* consequence which can follow, even if such a one conforms to another duty such as not killing. This difficulty, in fact, is one of the classic objections to deontology. Namely, what do we do when our duties conflict?

The attractions of deontological ethics to those who want to expunge uncertainty are obvious. They offer the obvious benefit of achieving certainty and the seemingly impervious satisfaction it bears, regardless of all evidences to the contrary. Some forms of pacifism, and there are many of them, are like this. Pacifists of principle, as they are often called, oppose any military actions regardless of all considerations by others which might be thought to justify them. Here the principle is all. There is nothing else. As I write, NATO is taking military action against the Serbs in Kosovo in the stated belief that it is justified in the avoidance of the greater evil posed by the Serbs' allegedly sustained massacre of Albanians. Given that the world is sadly like it is, there is no end of such dilemmas and they pose, directly and poignantly, the ancient conflict between those who would act only from a sense of intrinsic duty and those who believe, after due consideration, that such duty must give way to wider considerations in the pursuit of definable and desirable goals.

We will consider below some of the criticisms of deontological ethics posed by utilitarian ones, but for now we will, briefly, consider some other reasons why deontology is, in itself, now an inadequate approach to ethics.

Deontological ethics, as we have seen in passing, are notoriously negative. They are better at telling us what not to do than they are at the contrary. As a result, they inculcate a sense of moral virtue which is reactionary, rather than positive, and one, moreover, which is world denying rather than affirming. A further problem arises from this. Deontologists do not actually own the principles of their morality. Rather, they rely on being provided with them from a source of external authority, the unquestioning acceptance of which is made, by that authority, a condition of the virtue afforded. The principal danger of this is obvious. An ethically perverse authority, commanding such obeisance, can all too easily subvert moral virtue. Fascism of one sort or another is an obvious illustration of this, and it has often been observed that Nazism flourished in a Germanic culture over which Kant held much influence. The requirements of virtue can be changed, even subverted, with demonstrably frightening ease, given the 'right' socio-economic and political circumstances such as those which prevailed following the collapse of the Weimar Republic. Little wonder that the virtues, as deontologically defined, cause such unease and uncertainty. Little wonder, again, that the prevailing philosophical and moral mood after 1945 was so open to receive the exhortations of existentialist writers such as J-P. Sartre who argued that the only canon of moral virtue was that which required individual agents to own the responsibility for their actions. Sartre expressed this so firmly that he seemingly believed that even outrageous actions could be morally licit if the degree of the individual ownership of them was demonstrably high enough. More generally, the wider effect of post-1945 existentialist writing helped to produce a reactionary popular culture in which 'doing one's own thing' was lauded in song and action as a new liberation. Although this culture had within it the seeds of its own limitations, it did much to establish the widespread uncertainty which still prevails about the older deontological certainties, if for no other reasons than that they are of such antiquity and seemingly afford such assurance amid perplexity.

Another fundamental category which has long served and still appeals to those who seek certainty in ethics is that of natural law. This holds, briefly, that things are ethically right if they can be seen to be in accordance with what is thought to be natural as a consequence of observing the natural order. This view has played a prominent role in thinking about ethics from the time of the pre-Socratic philosophers to the present day. They used natural law as a basis for their definition of the civic virtues by trying to give all ethical terms a coherent meaning and, in so doing, define how people are to flourish in their natural state. Aristotle followed this, but importantly extended the notion to include all human beings and not just a few who were concerned about their privileged positions in the state. After him and prior to the Christian era, Cicero Latinized the Greek tradition with a formulation which stressed that there is one law for all which is eternal and unchangeable and its master is God 'for he is the author of this law, its promulgator and its enforcing judge'.[7]

There is a direct line from these pre-Christian natural law traditions to the present. In between there are, of course, many different traditions of natural law. What they have in common, however, is the belief that ethical virtue is somehow bound up with the observed order of nature. From this it followed that those who saw different purposes in nature invariably saw different interpretations of the laws which arose from their observations. Though their conclusions might be at variance as a result of their different observations, the methods used by different natural law thinkers are essentially the same, though it has been pithily observed that, 'the notion was laden with ambiguity even in the days when it was considered self-evident'.[8]

The history of the development of natural law from ancient Greece through the Christian tradition to the present is widely chronicled. The single most important figure in the latter is St Thomas Aquinas, who frequently quotes Cicero. Following Aristotle, Aquinas held that once we understand the purpose of our existence and the ends to which it is directed, then we can discover the means by which those ends are to be achieved. Aquinas put these Greek and Latin traditions together to produce his Christian account of natural law. He recognised four kinds of law: eternal, natural, human and divine. Natural law was the name he gave to the participation in divine law by rational creatures. He did not codify the laws, so understood, because he believed that they were so self-evident that all rational creatures could observe them for themselves by applying right reasoning to their experience. An example he gives of the laws so derived is that individuals should not do harm to one another. This and other such laws are what he called 'the impression of the divine light in us'. Such laws, he held, can change but they can never be abolished since they are part of the divine human encounter. Later writers on the subject stressed that such laws were more 'given' by God than observed by humans. Thomas Hobbes, for example, claimed that they were delivered by God in holy scriptures, rather than discovered by reason.

A modern example of natural law thinking which has caused no end of continuing debate can be found in the Papal Encyclical *Humanae Vitae*, published in 1968.[9] This, famously, forbade the use of artificial means of contraception on the grounds that it was unnatural. The emphasis here is on the word 'artificial' since the Encyclical did not proscribe the use of natural or 'rhythm' methods of contraception. The Encyclical is redolent with references to natural law. It lays down the rules given by God, which all God's creatures should keep. Such law, it claims, is enriched by God's own revelation. More recently, the Papal Encyclical *Veritatis Splendor* has addressed itself to the foundations of Roman Catholic moral theology. It does this by focusing on natural law as an order of nature which is accessible to all human beings and which is an expression of the divine providence.

From even this brief survey it can be seen how central natural law thinking is to Christian moral theology in particular and to Western culture in general. Again, however, it is for many no longer the source of certainty in ethics that it once was.

One central problem is that of *who* decides what is natural in the first place. What seems so to one might well not seem so to another. The former and abhorrent apartheid regime in South Africa used to be widely defended by arguing that it was 'natural', in the sense that birds of different species do not sit on the same branch! When we observe nature we, clearly, are as capable of reading things into it as we are out of it. As a consequence, so called natural laws are considered by many to be nothing but expressions of group self-interest. Philosophers have described such expressions as 'disguised stipulative definitions', meaning that observed laws are diktats read into nature rather than truths that are read out of it. Others have considered natural laws to be empirically falsifiable, tautologous or so general in their meaning as to be of little interest or real use.

The ancient debate about natural law will, of course, continue as we wrestle with the possibility that there is something about the very nature of things which is vital to our ethical well-being. Natural law boils down to something which may or may not be God-given, according to the view one takes, but something nevertheless which is either given in the way things actually are, or given in the way we understand them. An important contemporary debate here is that which seeks to base thinking about universal human rights in natural law theory. For our purpose, however, all we need observe is that natural law thinking no longer provides for many the indubitability in ethics that it once seemingly did and still does for some, such as those in the mainstream tradition of Roman Catholic moral theology as defined by *Humanae Vitae* and *Veritatis Splendor*.

A third methodology which we are now less sure about is utilitarianism. Extended discussion of this will follow in chapter 2. However, it needs to be considered briefly here so that we are clear about its shortcomings as an *ethical* theory. Ethical Utilitarianism is the view that ethical actions are to be considered right or wrong according to whether or not the consequences which arise from them are desirable or otherwise. This is, arguably, *the* great modern theory of ethics. There are two reasons for thinking this. First, it is not prefigured, as such, in antiquity in the sense that we have seen deonto-logical and natural law thinking to have been. Second, because it has had and still has immense influence for the simple reason that most people now instinctively think that the ethical acceptability or otherwise of our actions must be bound up, in some sense, with an assessment of the desirability, or otherwise, of the consequences which arise from them. This assumption is now widespread and implicit in the way ethical debates are conducted, particularly at a popular level.

The origin of ethical utilitarianism can be located with the publication in 1724 of Jeremy Bentham's *An Introduction to the Principles of Morals and Legislation* and specifically in its first four chapters.[10] He writes, 'Nature has placed mankind under the governance of two sovereign masters, *pain* and *pleasure*.' These govern everything we do and all attempts we might make to throw off our subjection to them are futile. The principle of utility is, simply, that by which we maximise pleasure and minimise pain. It is not, itself, susceptible of proof since it is the basis of everything else. 'A chain of proof', he writes, 'must have its commencement somewhere.' The principle is independent of the will of God and can for that reason be used as a test of whether that will is good or not. Moral goodness, so understood, is seen as a consequence of our actions and not as an intrinsic quality. Bentham added that straightforward scientific measurement could be used to apply the principle, by what he called his 'hedonic calculus'. By this means, he claims, it could be shown in advance whether or not a proposed action would promote pleasure or pain. This, in its simplicity, is what he called the 'greatest happiness' principle. As we will see in the next chapter, this strident, clear and secular theory of ethics has been hotly debated yet it continues to play a central part in both moral philosophy and popular thinking about morality. As mentioned above, it is so much a part of the modern world in which we live that we are all, whether we are always aware of it or not, to a large extent utilitarians in our thinking. All, that is, except some deontologists who are often vehement in their rejection of all forms of utilitarian thinking.

One obvious difficulty with ethical utilitarianism is that it places an awesome responsibility of calculus on the moral agent. Is it really possible for us, every time we make an ethical decision, to calculate its outcome in all the detail and with the certainty the theory requires? It might well be, of course, that in the development of the ethical life, individually and socially we accumulate confidence in this to such an extent that doing the right thing, so understood, becomes an intuitive second nature. This has been described as Rule-utilitarianism, to distinguish it from Act-utilitarianism in which the calculation literally has to be made in relation to each and every ethical act. Rule-utilitarianism is premised on the obvious fact that because many of our ethical decisions fall into categories, they can be rule governed, thus excusing us from the repeated burden of calculation in every instance of ethical perplexity. Here Rule-governed utilitarian morality manifests itself as collective ethical common sense, whatever 'collective' might mean in this context. One strength of such Rule-utilitarian thinking is that it can allow for the ways that different collectives might think about particular topics. That the mores of ethics vary from culture to culture and from time to time is widely acknowledged and accepted and the social dimension of rule-following undoubtedly helps us to cope with this. Clearly, even this brief consideration allows us to see that this slightly more sophisticated form of utilitarianism can be rendered in such a way as to free it from the obvious objections about the burdens of calculation. In this version, moreover, it seems to conform to normative ethics in the sense that it describes more or less what appears to happen when individuals make ethical decisions in a social context. Rule-utilitarianism can, therefore, be expected to appeal to any who want to accept the basic utilitarianism premises but free them from the first and most obvious objection.

Both these forms of utilitarian ethical theory, however, suffer from another and equally obvious difficulty. Namely, precisely what is a 'consequence' of an action? We live in a world of increasingly perceived complexity which often means that it is impossible for us ever to predict in advance just what the outcome of our actions will be. Indeed, the literature of tragedy is redolent with examples of those who acted with good intentions only to have to live with the tragic circumstances of the unforeseen outcomes of their actions. Such outcomes are invariably not singly identifiable. They are, rather, numerous and of ever-changing relationship to one another. As a result, some outcomes of a particular action might favour it, but others not. Utilitarian ethical theory has here, again, tried to meet this criticism by claiming that the ethical agent is only responsible for the *intended* outcomes of an action. A good example is that which occurs in military action when civilian casualties are incurred in attacks on military targets. Providing, this theory holds, these casualties were not *intended* in the first place and providing also, of course, that everything was done to avoid them, then the ethical agent cannot be held responsible. This is the so-called law of Double Effect in which it is acknowledged from the outset that the outcomes of our actions are multiple and not all equally desirable. Such intentionality is, however, an obscure area of philosophy to say the least. Precisely what is an intention? Is it a belief? Is it a claim to fore-knowledge? How can we know what another's intention actually is, particularly when it is disclosed *post eventum*?

Few, other than strict deontologists, would now claim rigorously that somehow or other and to some extent our ethical actions are not bound up with an assessment of the desirability or otherwise of the consequences to which they give rise. The view that they are, is part of what most people now instinctively think morality to be. The widespread extent to which this is the case is itself evidence of the all-pervading effect of post-eighteenth century modernity on modern culture. Utilitarian thinking is here and here to stay, notwithstanding its more obvious difficulties, which we have briefly considered. These remain, however, as common manifestations of uncertainty in ethics. We will see in the next chapter that such utilitarian thinking is the cause of yet more profound and widespread uncertainty in modern ethics even than these initial considerations might indicate.

A fourth and final methodology in modern ethics which we need to notice at this stage is the growing realisation that we cannot be laissez-faire about what we do in the belief that it will all be redeemed by some Hidden Hand of providence. Freedom of choice and expression, the essence of laissez-faire ethics and economics, is congenial to any, such as Christians, who want to emphasise the importance of free will. This, they argue, is the essence of what it means to be an individual and individuals alone are the source of all morality, even social morality. This view was notoriously put forward by Margaret Thatcher when she was the UK Prime Minister and said that there was 'no such thing as society'. Traditionally, Christians have drawn back from such a stark interpretation of the role of individualism in the collective ethical life. They have insisted, rather, that individuals need to act in concert with one another and out of a mutual concern for each other's best interests. Whereas, in classical laissez-faire economics, human freedom was tempered by the Hidden (and, for some, the divine) Hand, this tempering is now seen to be itself a part of human rather than divine responsibility. It should be noted, however, that for Adam Smith and his contemporaries, the belief in the Hidden Hand as a divine presence in human affairs genuinely gave the free market its ethical integrity. In the absence of such a belief, we now have to seek that integrity elsewhere. For this reason, the recurrent question now asked of the free market is: how much freedom should it be allowed and how do we exercise human constraint over it when we believe that it has reached the desirable limits of its freedom?

The demise of belief in the Hidden Hand in human affairs has itself been part of a wider rejection of belief in divine providence and this, again, has engendered uncertainty in modern ethics. We are no longer sure that all things will always turn out for the better. The general culture of evolutionary optimism which supported this view has itself collapsed with consequences we will consider in the next chapter. In its place there is a widespread awareness that we are, seemingly, on our own when we make ethical decisions. Later we will see that understanding of this is a precondition of understanding all our ethical decisions as 'acts of grace'. For now, all we need notice is the extent to which the awareness that there is seemingly no 'fall back' position if we get things wrong economically is a cause of widespread uncertainty in ethics. This is compounded by the further realisation that our economic woes are, in fact, political ones at root and we know just how seemingly impossible it often is to solve these.

Whilst all the foregoing ethical concepts no longer afford, for the majority, access to certainty in morality for reasons such as those we have discussed, they nevertheless remain central to ethical debate. They will be found, for example, throughout contemporary discussions of the subject and all have their apologists. Indeed, writers on ethics can more or less be grouped according to the views they take in relation to these central issues. They will, therefore, remain central to ongoing debates. All we have noticed here are the principal reasons why they no longer afford the certainty in ethics which they once apparently did for many and still seem to do for some.

There are at least three further readily identifiable reasons why uncertainty manifests itself in ethics and we will now consider these briefly before looking at the origins of this uncertainty in the next chapter.

The first is the uncertainty caused by the sheer complexity of our knowledge of the natural order. Whereas in the quite recent past we divided such knowledge into academic disciplines, we are no longer able to do so with the same certainty. These older disciplines frequently merge into each other and often scarcely seem able to account for the complexity of the phenomena we observe. In physics, for example, chaos theory now reigns where only recently all was talk of order and predictability. As a result, physicists now have to come to terms with otherwise quite random and previously entirely unexpected associations. The same is true of the medical sciences. Whereas it was recently believed, with good reason, that major advances had been made in conquering widespread diseases with treatments such as antibiotics, the emergence of new strains of disease such as AIDS which are caused by retro-viruses and which are known to be treatment resistant, pose a considerable threat to public health. We are confronted with the complexity of these phenomena when we thought they were simple. This leads to the second cause of the now widespread uncertainty which impinges upon ethics. This is the awareness of the limitations of our knowledge.

To our constant embarrassment, our knowledge is now often seemingly at its weakest where we most need it to be strong. As we have seen, in the current debate about the acceptability or otherwise of genetically modified crops, we are apparently at a complete loss to know if they will be beneficial or not, whether we can do without them or not, or if they will unleash new genes which will destroy existing unmodified ones and thereby destabilise the 'balance' of nature. None of this information is, in fact, available to us and we are left with opinions of one sort or another which are often clearly motivated by vested interests. The same is true of our new abilities to clone living tissue. We are, rightly no doubt, scared about the implication of cloning human beings, but want to remain open to the possibility that cloned tissue for surgery and other purposes could bring immense human benefits. Here, again, our knowledge is effectively non-existent in an area where there are pressing ethical questions to be answered. Examples of the same could be multiplied across innumerable areas of contemporary science in which we simply do not have the knowledge we require to enable us to answer simple questions about the morality, or otherwise, of using the little knowledge we have acquired. Moreover, we know that this state of affairs is unlikely to change radically. Whilst our knowledge does, of course, advance dramatically and frequently in specific areas, it nevertheless remains insufficient to the scale of the problem. The plain truth is that we will never know at any one time all that we need to know to solve our pressing ethical problems. A complete answer to everything is as elusive as it ever was and ever will be. Some scientists, it is true, think that there may well be such an explanation awaiting us just around the corner and that it might well be more simple than we can imagine. But it remains to be wondered if this hope tells us more about the hubris of science and scientists than it does about the mysteries of the world in which we live. How curious these aspirations now seem. How vain, even, they remain in the face of our acute awareness of the limitation of our knowledge.

None of this means that we should despair, or fail to increase our knowledge by every means available. On the contrary, immense benefits have accrued as a result of the expansion of our knowledge in the modern world and we can have every confidence that they will continue to do so. This does and will happen most frequently at the limits of our technologies as we both expand their capabilities and invent ever new ones. It is well to remember, however, that such technologies are human artefacts in just the sense that the primitive tools of our ancestors were. For this reason alone it is unwise for us to think that we are that much in advance of them in these crucial areas. Our technologies, like theirs, exist at the limits of our abilities and, more to the point, bear the hallmarks of us their creator. All human artefacts therefore reflect human nature and in particular its capacity for good and evil. Time and again our inventions can be put to good and evil use for the simple reason that they have built into them, as artefacts, our own capacities for good and evil. The sobering truth about this is that, as human beings, we will never be able to make anything of unalloyed goodness because of the flaws in our nature.

We began by reflecting on how ethical problems have human, factual and religious/philosophical manifestations. To these must now be added the manifestation of uncertainty for the sort of reasons we have now also considered. Such uncertainty is, so to speak, a further fact we have to take into account if we are to come to terms with what it means to live the ethical life. It is now, moreover, something which is likely to feature more and more rather than less as we seek, in all areas of life, to do the right thing. The reason for this is that behind the manifestations of uncertainty we have briefly considered, there lie irreversible religious, philosophical and cultural trends.

It remains to be said, importantly, that predominant though uncertainty now is in modern life and particularly in ethics, and need to face it though we must, we should not, however, always consider it to be a bad thing in itself. Uncertainty in the future inculcates a respectful attitude towards it. This alone suffices to remind us that our mastery of the future is never absolute and never can be. At the very least this requires of us a certain humility in the estimation of our own powers. It can therefore be helpful in encouraging individual effort, as anyone who has ever prepared for an examination or similar tough assignment, or great adventure of any kind, will know only too well. It also lies behind the most successful (admittedly according to a personal view and only when it is subject to proper controls) system of economics the world has ever seen: the market economy. Uncertainty encourages initiative and competition. It also produces capital for investment and the expectation of its increase. Uncertainty is also what inspires artistic endeavour as artists seek to break new ground. Most extremely, the uncertainty of danger itself is a source of healthy attraction. It is what so often inspires human beings to test their endurance and capacities and what provides the source of heroism.

Uncertainty can also be socially cohesive, as is manifestly demonstrated whenever human beings collectively face common threats and enemies. Examples of this from wartime are the most obvious, but making common cause against uncertainty is also a healthy feature of more everyday life. It brings people together and focuses their efforts. It also reminds us that we can so often work better together than individually. Indeed, as we have seen and without too much reflection, it is possible to identify obvious social benefits deriving from uncertainty. Even if they turn out to be illusory rather than actual, there are so many of them that probability alone suggests that the overall effect must be beneficial. It has also been noted that uncertainty is beneficial for democracy.[11] This argument, again, is a simple one. Politicians in democracies know that there is only one thing certain about their own futures, their very uncertainty. Daily they have to face their colleagues, the electorate and, increasingly for good or ill, the press. Not for nothing did Harold Wilson, former UK Labour Prime Minister, memorably say: 'A week is a long time in politics.' All this can, of course, lead to weak democratic governments and hand-to-mouth political survival. This is why some stability and term-future is so necessary in democratic systems. Without working majorities parties cannot see through terms of office and programmes of political, economic and other reform. But then, again, single party dominance is also equally bad for democracy.

For these reasons uncertainty is a not totally undesirable fact of life and it can be the thing that gives it spice and makes it worth living. None of this is being denied or lamented here. Indeed it would not be difficult to reflect at much more length on the virtues and blessings of uncertainty. All we have drawn attention to is the fact that we seemingly now face inordinate degrees of uncertainty in our ethical lives; individually and collectively. In the next chapter, we will examine the reasons which lie behind this and which indicate to us that the situation is not going to change because they are inextricably bound up with our Western age and culture as well as being universally significant. In chapter 3, we will see that recourse to certainty in religions like Christianity is no solution to the problem. Only after that will we be able to approach the subject from an alternative Christian point of view which addresses the situation as, by then, we will have understood it.

Chapter Two

The Origins of Modern Ethical Uncertainty

There is nothing particularly unique about our modern *ethical* uncertainty for the simple reason that, as Kenneth Galbraith memorably reminded us, we live in an 'age of uncertainty'.[1] This has been variously described and its origins much speculated upon. For our purpose, however, we will locate the roots of our modern ethical uncertainty in the eighteenth century; in what has been described as 'the Enlightenment project'. The attempt, that is, to find a new basis for politics, jurisprudence and, above all, ethics. One that is based on rationally demonstrable principles, rather than assumption, presupposition, authority, habit and custom. In all this, a genuinely new mood of modernity was born. Two things principally made it possible: rapidly changing political circumstances and new philosophical discoveries in epistemology (the study of what we can know and how we do so) and ontology (the study of how things exist). Which of these precipitated the other, the changing politics or the new philosophy, is debatable but need not detain us. For convenience, we will look briefly at the changing political mood and then examine the new philosophy at more length, in order to see why it is that our modern uncertainty was, in fact, implicit within it from the beginning. Following that we will look at three other reasons which lie behind our modern ethical uncertainty; geopolitical, ecological and scientific ones.

Eighteenth century northern Europe was, as is well known, an area of growing social unrest. The Industrial Revolution had brought people with common interests together as never before. To meet this need, modern cities for the most part just happened, very few were planned. People who had previously only known rural isolation and with that the comparatively non-existent opportunities for collective representation and action, now found themselves in possession of a new power, based on those very things which had become available simply by dint of the fact that they lived and worked together in hitherto unprecedented large numbers. This made rapid communication between them possible, and that in turn facilitated the expression of a common will on topics of shared interest; in particular, those concerning working and living conditions. Some industrialists, of course, responded by doing all they could to provide acceptable working and living conditions, but for the most part people were left to look after their own interests in an adversarial relationship with their employers, who were invariably also their landlords and purveyors of one sort or another. For these simple reasons, the Industrial Revolution had the seeds of revolution built into its social and economic fabric. Things were clearly going to have to change and none more so than established political orders. Merrie England had gone for ever. The self-improvement and education of the working classes, so much a feature of the next century, was long off and the general mood remained largely inarticulate though its presence and latent power was evident to all. Little wonder that in England, at least, the general mood was ripe for harvest by evangelical revivalist preachers such as the Wesley brothers and others. Although it was not, of course, their primary intention, it has often been observed that the success of religious revivalism did much in England to prevent the fomenting of social unrest that was to lead to revolution in France and elsewhere. The old agrarian order had gone for ever and taken with it the social and economic institutions which had supported it for centuries. A revisionist approach to politics came out of all this essentially political upheaval. It was a century or so in the coming and did not reach the statute in England, for example, until the Great Reform Bill of 1832, which, by then, had other socially pressing needs behind it such as the need to maintain law and order following the return of large numbers of people to civilian life after the end of the Napoleonic wars.

The foundations for harnessing all this potential in a new political economy were, strangely perhaps, not laid until 1848 when Karl Marx and Friedrich Engels wrote the Communist Manifesto, and the attempt to create that economy did not happen until 1917.[2] As a philosopher, rather than political economist, Marx knew that the key to social and economic improvement was a remarkably simple thing: human freedom. His simple point was that what human beings had made they could also change, and change by revolution if necessary.

This brief excursus into social and economic history has been necessary simply to remind us that the philosophical revolutions of the eighteenth century, to which we will now turn, were themselves part of a much wider phenomenon which was nothing less than the origin of a new social, political and economic order. They were also premised upon an immediately preceding interest in philosophical rationalism, the principal author of which was the philosopher René Descartes (1596–1650) who can with some confidence be described as the first modern philosopher. This rationalism had two main features. First, it was scientific in its method in the sense that it wanted to know about the actual, rather than the supposed, nature of things. Second, following Descartes, it distinguished between the knowing subject and the external world. This is now such a commonplace, even in everyday and ordinary understandings of things, that we are scarce able to imagine what a powerful new idea it effectively became through the pen of Descartes. Its political potential was, of course, later exploited by Marx and others. Descartes also emphasised the simple point that philosophy should always begin *de novo*. Nothing should be taken for granted, and this is the point, regardless of the authority by which it might have been established. Little wonder that the new rationalists, devoutly religious though many of them were, were to come into such conflict with religious authorities. The starting point for all progress in philosophy, according to Descartes, was his famous *cogito ergo sum*, I think therefore I am. The indubitability of consciousness was, for Descartes, the foundation stone of philosophy and the source of all knowledge; the only thing that could be taken as being axiomatic without further question. This effective redefinition of the nature of knowledge and the task of philosophy set its modern agenda.

Amid all the eighteenth-century philosophical rationalists who followed where Descartes had led, Jeremy Bentham stands out as the one, more than any other, who captured a vision of the implications of the new philosophy for the new political mood. He was also a talented writer, able to communicate his ideas lucidly and concisely. This he did to great effect in the first four chapters of his *An Introduction to the Principles of Morals and Legislation,* first published in 1734. The immediate and lasting influence of this text cannot be overestimated and it stands as one of the all-time great examples of the direct effect of philosophical thinking on every area of life and thought. We have already seen in chapter 1 why ethical utilitarianism is now susceptible to criticisms which generate uncertainty in modern ethics. We will now consider in more detail why these uncertainties were implicit in the philosophy from its inception.

Bentham, was a rationalist in the clear sense that he believed that rational powers were, in themselves, sufficient both for challenging tradition and for creating alternatives to it in morals and legislation. Whilst such rationality is, of course, important and will ever remain so, the utter self-confidence with which Bentham and others exercised it is no longer available to us. Bentham thought that the fundamentals of his system were axiomatic in the sense that they needed no further proof. In this he was followed a century later by his disciple John Stuart Mill. He, however, was acutely aware that not all pleasures were equal in the sense that Bentham had supposed they were for the purposes of comparison and calculation and that, as a result, the unquestioning confidence with which Bentham exercised his calculus needed defending against criticism by those who felt that 'lower' pleasures could not be compared directly with 'higher' ones. There is, Mill acknowledged, a distinction between them and, to that extent at least, he accepted the criticism. But, and this is the point, he was unable to explain how the distinction was to be made beyond suggesting that 'competent judges' would do this.[3] In other words, these people, whoever they were, would make their own subjective distinctions just as aesthetes have ever done. In centrally doubting Bentham's definition of happiness in this way, Mill, in effect, doubted everything else his master had written. Whatever else morality was to be based upon, it could not be based on calculation, at least not in the way Bentham had envisaged.

The effect of all this on Bentham's stridently self-confident theory was to rob it of its claims of objectively demonstrable certainty in an area where it most depended on them. The whims of the administrators, the purveyors of *ipse dixits*, had now reinfiltrated the very system of ethics which was designed in the first place to put them out of business. Opinionating had not been expunged, and to that extent, Bentham's bold experiment had failed. It could no longer demonstrate solely according to its initial principles how particular courses of action were preferable to others on the ground that they maximised some objectively quantified amount of pleasure or happiness for the majority of people. Did they? And if so how? And who was to decree this on behalf of the many in the first place? The problems with a theory such as this are legion. As we also saw briefly in the last chapter, none of these difficulties killed it off. Far from it. The belief that in some way the moral acceptability or otherwise of our proposed actions is bound up with an assessment of the acceptability or otherwise of their consequences is now almost universally acknowledged. But we are not as confident as Bentham in being sure how this is the case. He believed, with others incidentally, that the so-called wider Philosophical Radicalism of which his system was part had discovered 'laws' pertaining to associationism in psychology that demonstrated the links between ideas and their outcomes akin to the 'laws' Newton had discovered in physics and therefore of the same status. We know, of course, that this was not the case and such associationist psychology has long been discredited, but it did play a vital part in establishing the initial credibility of Bentham's system.

In an influential critical assessment of what he calls 'the Enlightenment project', Alasdair Macintyre criticises Bentham and others on the simple ground that they had no vision of human nature as it ought to be: a vision which was held in pre-Christian Greek classical systems of ethics, as well as, almost universally, by Christian ones up to the eighteenth century and still by many to this day.[4] Without such a vision, Macintyre argues, the real business of morality, of getting people from where they are to where they ought to be, cannot even be started. He observes, as we have done, that the new social setting of the eighteenth century was crucial in all that and adds that it was responsible for the virtual invention of the central role of the individual in morality, with a new and unprecedented status in ethical theo-rising. Such individuals were, according to Bentham, possessed of incredible powers of enlightened rational calculation untainted by their shortcomings as individuals. To say this belief was also naively optimistic in its view of human nature is but to state the obvious in the light of the atrocities which humans have inflicted upon each other in the twentieth century. Clearly, something more profound is needed here. Something which will not deny the awesomely creative powers of individuals nor the extent to which they can and should use their rational powers, but something that also takes wider considerations about individual and collective human nature into deeper account. We will return to this in later chapters, but for now will examine other reasons why the roots of uncertainty lie deep in the eigh-teenth-century Enlightenment.

We have briefly seen something of the extent to which Bentham's system of ethics relied on the powers of rationality, or the certainty with which things like the outcomes of our proposed actions could be predicted. Did he, we must ask, push the Cartesian certainties further than they were capable of? Did he make too much of the freedom individuals acquired once they had distinguished their existence from that of the world around them? The work of at least two other eighteenth-century philosophers would suggest that he certainly did this and that he was in error as a result. They are the Scottish philosopher David Hume and the German philosopher that he inspired,

Immanuel Kant. We will now briefly consider why the writing of both these influential thinkers laid further foundations for modern ethical uncertainty.

The Scottish empiricist philosopher David Hume (1711–1776) was famous for exposing the limits of empiricism, of what we can actually know. Bentham, as we have seen, confidently thought that there was substance to the self and to the association of ideas with action. Hume attacked these and other rationalist presumptions so successfully that he has, effectively, never been answered. He began by distinguishing between ideas and impressions. The latter are what we experience when we feel heat, cold, pleasure or pain. 'Ideas' is the name he gives to the subsequent recall of those impressions. These are less forceful than impressions. 'All ideas,' he writes, 'especially abstract ones, are naturally faint and obscure.'[5] He further distinguished between simple ideas and complex ones. The former are what clearly arise from an impression in the sense that they correspond with it. The latter might be based on impressions but they invariably go beyond them and thereby enter the sphere of the imagination. All complex ideas, however, are based on simple ones. We cannot, therefore, know anything which is not derived, at least in part, from some impression which had created a simple idea. We cannot, he concludes from this, ever transcend the scant knowledge we derive for our impressions and the simple ideas we derive from them, complex though these might later become in the uses we put them to. He made another, for our purpose important, distinction. It is that between what he calls 'relations of ideas' and 'matters of fact'.[6] Relations of ideas are what constitute the sciences of geometry, algebra and arithmetic. All comprise thought operations which bear no necessary relation to or 'dependence on what is anywhere existent in the universe'.[7] Matters of fact are quite otherwise and are not capable of being demonstrated with the same indubitability. The evidence for their truth is, therefore, not to be compared. Matters of fact, he added, were derived from our experiences of cause and effect. 'By means of that relation alone we can go beyond the evidence of our memory and senses.' He concludes from this that 'causes and effects are discoverable, not by reason but by experience'.[8] Hume is, however, extremely cautious about identifying the basis of our knowledge from experience and concludes 'even after we have experience of the operations of cause and effect, our conclusions from that experience are *not* founded on reasoning or any process of the understanding'.[9] If we say, therefore, that *X causes Y* we are not saying that we know anything about *X and its relationship with Y* that leads us to that conclusion. We can deduce nothing from the 'cause' beyond that fact that we so frequently observe it to be the case that we expect it to be so. From this Hume famously concluded that 'causation exists in the mind and not objects'. This is because there is no certain route from the experience based on observation to the idea of causation. We associate the latter with the former but that is all we can do. Having thus dismantled the philosophical credibility of causation, Hume turned his attention to the 'self'. Here again he came to notoriously negative conclusions, abolishing substance just as he had done causation. We cannot know anything about the substance of the self, he claims, since all we can know about ourselves is derived from a series of sensations beyond which we cannot penetrate. This conclusion had two important consequences: it abolished substance from psychology and it denied the possibility of us ever having knowledge of the human soul, or whatever other name we give to what is essentially human.

This brief excursus into Hume's epistemology has been necessary for us to understand what a critical impact it had on eighteenth-century rationalism and theology. What Hume did was to show that the very premises on which rationalism was based did not lead to the conclusions rationalists invariably came to. Rationalists who were then active and predominant in theology, psychology and ethics effectively had the ground cut from under their feet by a contemporary, or a near one. His principal application of all this to ethics concluded that we cannot get to ethical approval or disapproval from anything reason can establish. He famously argues, as a result of this conclusion, that we can never form opinions about what *ought* or *ought not* to be the case from observation of what *is* or *is not* the case. Attempts to do this he dubbed as the 'naturalistic fallacy' and if it were but avoided, he argued, then all the vulgar systems of morality could be subverted.[10] Morality, he concluded, 'was more properly felt than judged of'.[11] Virtues cannot, therefore, be justified rationally as Bentham and others argued, nor can they be based upon factual knowledge of any kind as theologians, among others, were wont to argue. They could only be *felt*. Social virtue is therefore, for Hume, a disposition. He writes, 'It appears that a tendency to public good, and to the promoting of peace, harmony and order in society, does always, by affecting the benevolent principles of our frame, engage us on the side of the social virtues.'[12] In considerable sympathy here with Bishop Butler and against the empirical rationalists, Hume concludes that humankind possesses a disposition to do good and avoid evil. His argument here made much of the fact that humans acted morally towards each other and together because they possessed a 'sympathy' for each other which was the source of their mutuality. Those unsympathetic to others are incapable of knowing or exercising virtue whereas 'on the other hand, it is always found, that warm concern for the interests of our species is attended with a delicate feeling of all moral distinctions'.[13] In this way, moral goodness is derived from human experience and not from reason. Unlike Butler, however, Hume did not have recourse to a theological understanding of moral perversity. For Hume the pursuit of goodness was a matter of trusting to the givenness of one's instincts in seeking the civil society. This made him a somewhat conservative thinker on particular ethical issues since such a position obviously favours the status quo and thereby inculcates ethical conservatism. He did not, for example, much like social reform on the grounds that removal of public enemy number one would simply make room for the promotion of number two and no net improvement would therefore result. It is irresistible to wonder here if Hume did not actually enjoy his iconoclasm to the point of irony.

Hume thus created an epistemology in which all the certainties on which others had premised their rationality and morality were shown to be false. On the slender foundation of minimalism of perception in epistemology and sympathy in morality Hume created his own theories of both. All belief in the reality and permanence of these things is swept away, but will creep back and create delusion if we fail to be vigilant. Whether or not this radical empirical scepticism is convincing, or even to our liking, is beside the important point for our purposes. All we need to notice is that enlightenment rationalism was, at very least, based on philosophical assumptions which could be demonstrably falsified. For that reason alone, it could no longer be considered the bastion of rational certainty which it had to be to accomplish and succeed in its undertakings. As we will see below, subsequent and much more recent developments in the philosophy of science have echoed Hume's scepticism and, in so doing, have brought again to the fore an awareness of uncertainty in areas of epistemology which were once thought impervious to it.

Our main purpose for discussing Hume in this way has been to show that such uncertainty was, at least arguably and from his point of view, endemic in the Enlightenment project from the beginning. Hume did not destroy belief and morality, that would be an impossibility, what he did was to show that they were to be located in our feelings and not our cognitive powers. They were no less real because of this, but the truth about them could not be established in the manner that the rationalists had so firmly believed. Hume's sceptical challenges to them still ring down the centuries and remain, in their turn, as difficult to answer as they ever were. For all that, however, there was still a confidently held and widespread belief that there was an external world out there and that it was somehow related to morality. Until some better explanation was found, therefore, the account of that world given by the traditional rationalists prevailed, even if only for want of a better one. But there was even greater difficulty for the rationalists not far ahead. This time it came from Germany, but it was related to this Scottish challenge by David Hume for the simple reason that it was this that 'awoke' the German philosopher Immanuel Kant from his self-described dogmatic slumbers. Kant saw that Hume had 'inferred the nullity of all pretentions of reason to advance beyond the empirical'.[14] He realised that 'if we accept his [Hume's] conclusions, then all that we call metaphysics is a mere delusion whereby we fancy ourselves to have rational insight into what, in actual fact, is borrowed solely from experience, and under the influence of custom has taken the illusory semblance of necessity.'[15] As we will now see, Kant effectively finished the job begun by Hume and in so doing colluded with him in showing that the certainties premised on the external world were as false as those based on claims to rational knowledge.

Kant's influence on understandings of philosophy, theology and ethics in the modern world cannot be overestimated. According to some interpreters, his influence was so great that theology had to be reconstructed, beginning immediately after him with the work of Frederich Schleiermacher who for that reason is often called the father of modern theology. In turn, new theologies emerged in Germany and England which were distinctive enough to be recognised as 'post-Kantian'. In the mid-nineteenth century they caused great controversies in England, but our view of those has, in retrospect at least, been overshadowed by the contemporaneous Darwinian ones. The influence of this theology is vigorous in contemporary debates which continue to focus on the nature and status of our knowledge of God, which, as we shall see, were central Kantian concerns.

Kant, a native of Königsberg, was a philosophy teacher of considerable wit whose writings are all based on his lecture notes. For this reason, it is of passing interest to note that in this sense he was a modern working and teaching philosopher, rather than one who wrote for a readership at a remove. Would that we could know more than we do about the effect that lively debate with students had on the development of his thought. We do know that he revised his lectures constantly, (a fact which often makes the interpretation of his thought the more difficult), and can but imagine how this came about in the midst of his busy and methodical life. There is scarcely a better example of how one philosopher can, by working assiduously, have such world-shattering influence. For our purpose we will primarily consider the first of his three great Critiques, *The Critique of Pure Reason*. This first appeared in 1781, but we will use the second and, for the reasons we have considered, revised edition of 1787.

With a lack of false modesty, which might of course have been feigned simply to entertain his students (every lecturer knows this old trick!), Kant claimed that what was needed and what this *Critique* provided was nothing less than a 'Copernican Revolution' in philosophy. He writes of this:

> Hitherto it has been assumed that all our knowledge must conform to objects. But all attempts to extend our knowledge of objects by establishing something in regard to them *a priori*, by means of concepts, have, on this assumption, ended in failure. We must therefore make trial whether we may not have more success in the tasks of metaphysics, if we suppose that objects must conform to knowledge.[16]

The implications of this revolution, for theology at least, are immediately obvious. No longer should we seek to conform our knowledge to God's existence, what we must do, rather, is to ask how that existence conforms to our knowledge. But before we explore that in more depth, we need to notice in a little more detail what it was about Kant's philosophy which destroyed certainty in ontology in the way Hume had done in epistemology. 'Ontology', literally 'the study of being', is one of the central studies of philosophy for the simple reason that we live in a material world which has all the appearance of existing independently of ourselves. Natural curiosity, at the very least, causes us to enquire into the manner of that existence. It was in this very task that Kant claimed we could not make any real progress, for the again simple reason that the experience of that world was itself a form of knowledge 'which involves understanding; and understanding has rules which I must presuppose as being in me prior to objects being given to me, and therefore as being *a priori*'. [17] To this Kant added the observation that because we can never transcend the limits of our experience, we can only know of metaphysical objects through that experience and (which is the main point to notice for our purpose) can never know them as they-are-in-themselves. He writes 'we can…have no knowledge of any object as a thing in itself, but only in so far as it is an object of sensible intuition, that is, an appearance.' All this had the obvious effect of banishing substance from philosophy in general and ontology in particular. Kant did not deny that the external world existed, all he insisted upon is that we have no way of demonstrating that it does so that is not subject to the limitation of our powers as knowing subjects. To appreciate a little more clearly the impact of this for theology it is first necessary to understand the distinction Kant made between two types of proposition. These he termed 'analytic' and 'synthetic' respectively.

In the first case, the predicates are contained in, and can therefore be derived from, the subjects. For example, if we say that a ball is 'round' we have said something analytic in the sense that the predicate 'round' is contained in the subject 'ball'. In this case the predicate adds nothing to the subject. If, however, we say that the ball is 'green' then we have added something to the subject, thereby creating a synthesis. Again, the application of this to theology is obvious. Kant claimed that 'existence' is not a predicate which adds anything to its subject for the simple reason that 'existence' is implied in the subjects to begin with. To say therefore, that 'God exists' is to say nothing about God. With characteristic humour Kant points out that using 'existence' in this way is like adding noughts to one's bank account; it makes no difference. In his well known critical discussion of the famous medieval five arguments for the existence of God, Kant points out that they all depend on one, the so-called ontological argument which claims that God's existence is a necessity. Kant argues, rather, that such existence is an unintelligibility.

Before we consider briefly the implications of Kant's Copernican revolution for ethics, all we need note here is that Kant, with immense influence, banished the possibility of substance playing any part in philosophy independent of the manner in which we perceive it. This, as we shall see again below, was to become one of the other great philosophical reasons for creating uncertainty in modern culture generally. We will now consider how this, according to Kant, applied to ethics.

His main work on this subject is *The Groundwork of the Metaphysic of Morals,* first published in 1783. What he, in effect, does is to re-create certainty in morality within the limits of knowledge as he had defined them. He begins with the claim that there is only one thing which is unconditionally good and that is a 'good will'. From this it follows that Kantian ethical values are volitional in the sense that we will them into, rather than infer them from, existence. Duty is derived from the exercise of will alone. It is a principle of volition. We discover what this is by subjecting ethical propositions to the test of universalisability. We are to act dutifully, therefore, if and only if we will our maxim to become a universal law of nature. If, that is, we will that everyone else should always act in the same way in the same situation. If the answer to this is 'yes' then the maxim becomes what Kant called a 'categorical imperative'. Such an imperative in Kantian philosophy is *a priori* in the sense that it is independent of any particular experience and because it is equally binding on everyone. Elsewhere in his writing Kant famously claimed that whilst morality, so understood, did not depend upon religion it, nevertheless, led ineluctably to it. For Kant, therefore, morality required religion rather than religion required morality.

All this is generally relevant to our discussion, but the main point for us to note is that Kantian philosophy in general treated religion and ethics centrally and it did so in a way which first required the denial of the older certainties on which those subjects were invariably premised. Many continued, and still do, to reject Kant's revolution and rely on the certainties he denied, but the power of his denial is, as mentioned above, a reverberating one with the result that theology can still be divided broadly into that which dates from Kant and Schleiermacher and that which is still more noticeably coterminous with older traditions and certainties which pre-dated them.

We have now seen why, for two philosophical reasons, epistemological and ontological, uncertainty was an intrinsic element of the Enlightenment in spite of all the claims it made to the contrary about its rational certainties and the wider confidences they created. We will now look briefly at three other reasons which lie behind our age of uncertainty and which bear, in particular, on our ethical uncertainty. They are, in turn, geopolitical uncertainty, ecological uncertainty, and scientific uncertainty.

Earlier we saw in passing that the term 'post-modern' is used in numerous ways, but that it is probably most frequently used to describe the changed state-of-affairs which was brought about by the eighteenth-century Enlightenment. It has also been used to describe the altered situation after the end of the Second World War in 1945. This was in an essay by Francis Fukuyama entitled 'The End of History'. Nicholas Boyle, in a recent discussion of this, notes that the essay argues that after 1945 a new world order came into existence.[18] This was one which saw the end of empires and of the cultural self-confidence on which they had been built. It is difficult for us now to imagine what the geopolitical map was like in even the historically recent past when the world was divided up between the empires of nation states who proudly coloured their atlases for the purposes of propaganda and education. The last of these to collapse was, of course, the Soviet one in 1989. With that gone, the way in which nations relate to each other internationally is quite different, with the United Nations

Organisation playing an increasingly prominent role. Fukuyama claims that 1989 completed a process heralded in 1945 and that things after really were going to be different, for the simple reason that no other such geopolitical change could possibly equal the collapse of the Soviet system. Boyle reflects ironically at this point on the many previous such occasions when people have been erroneously confident that nothing could ever change the world so much as it had changed and then was. If nothing else, this clearly reflects a deep longing people have in all cultures and at all times for social, economic and political stability. Prior to 1989, Boyle observes, the economic order had already been changing in seeming anticipation. Global trade dominated by multinational organisations had been coming into existence ready to emerge when the time was ripe as it then clearly was. Boyle thinks that this was the trigger of post-modernism, the changed economic order that 1945 and 1989 made possible rather than those dates as such. Perhaps even 1989 was itself the result rather than the cause of that, as the West by then had clearly won the nuclear arms race in the sense that it was able, seemingly at least, to afford ever more expensive weapons systems, such as 'Star Wars' so beloved by President Reagan, and the Soviets were not.

The older world order in which nations and their allies controlled the world stage was clearly a familiar one and it was envisaged, even after 1945, at the Yalta conference and elsewhere, that that would continue. Indeed the anticipation that that would be the case clearly influenced the events at the end of the war when, following the imminence of the German collapse, the Western and Soviet allies vied with each other to claim the imminently vacant territories. But the new demography was not to last and the world really was going to be different. Whilst these events were undoubtedly sensationally described as the 'end of history', that title does, as we have seen, make an important point. Things are very different. Although the possibility of global military confrontation has, thankfully, receded we are now threatened by innumerable local civil unrests which we barely know how to deal with. The UN, by common consent, has a 'peacekeeping' role, but there is uncertainty about how that should be exercised. As a result, the international community often has to stand by helplessly as serious disorders perpetuate suffering on unimaginable local scales. A further issue relates to this. The new world order requires that nations answer to its rule by opening their weapons systems to international inspection and control. It takes just one nation to fail in this respect, for the international order to be wrong-footed and even divided, as is currently happening with Iraq through the effect that that nation is having on the UN Security Council.

The overall impact of these and other events, such as the now rapidly escalating influence of the European Union and its economic significance, is the emergence of yet further and widespread uncertainty. We simply do not know what the newly emerging world order will be like, or how the bit of it we happen to belong to will fit into the whole. We do know that the new world order will be interdependent as never before and that this will be for environmental and other, as well as military, reasons. The way we all live anywhere on the planet now affects the way everyone else on it lives and we scarcely have recourse to the political institutions which can effectively regulate that. It is salutary for us to remember that our now ever-present global environmental consciousness is a very recent thing; so recent that many think it dates from the space-age and particularly from when we were all arrested by pictures of the earth as an oasis in seemingly vast and probably hostile space. At the very least, this effected a new international and trans-cultural sense of interdependence. From out there, our differences down here seemed so trivial in comparison with the difference we all shared with space as it was newly perceived. This is arguably yet another source of our modern uncertainty. Our perceptions, then, of our common lot, are different from even those of our preceding generations and in their many ways they lie behind our very real sense of uncertainty. We are, therefore, seemingly well justified in thinking that our situation is so different that it will require answers to problems which are also different in the sense that they will not have been prefigured. This, of course, is what the post-modernists claim, but we have already considered why this response of 'presentism' needs to be tempered with a consistently open attitude to that past and how it can still come to our aid. We will return to that in later chapters.

Our ecological uncertainties follow on from those just discussed and, for reasons we will consider, are particularly poignant for religious believers. They arise from the awareness we now have of the potential instability of our eco-system and from the knowledge that its life is time-limited. It cannot last for ever, at least in a way that will sustain life as we now know it. We also know that our appearance on the world stage is late in time. The universe and the bit of it we occupy, it is commonly agreed, is some fifteen billion years old. The life-chain of which we are part emerged only some seven million years ago and the particular form of it we call human dates from our Cro-Magnon ancestors who came into Europe, probably out of Africa, only some thirty thousand years ago. These figures are staggering. Little wonder that we ask by what right we are here and by what further right we can expect to stay. Religions have, of course, answered this in their own profound ways. They all contain some explanation of why we are here, what we should do about it, and what we can expect to happen in the future. The Jewish and Christian traditions were marked for most of their history with a belief in the relatively recent creation of the earth (only in the sixteenth century did the devout and scholarly Archbishop of Armagh date the creation to 4,004 BCE, and he was widely believed up to the nineteenth century), as well as by a further belief that it would come to an end in God's good time. The adjustment of Christianity to an acceptance of the permanence of history, however, took place early in its life. The adjustment to the acceptance of the extreme antiquity of the world has by comparison, of course, been a painful and slow one in the last century or so, since Darwin's theories have become irrefutable at least in their outline. For this reason, Christianity has had to go through an incredible shift of understanding in order to maintain its credibility in the greater part of the modern world.

For as long as the world was thought to be of recent origin and of a certain future, it was possible to maintain the belief that it was sustained in the way it was by a loving Creator for that Creator's purposes. The doctrinal name for this was 'providence' and it plays a prominent role in Jewish and Christian history. Under its influence, Jews and Christians alike have believed that their destiny was safe in the hands of a loving creator. They have even believed, and many still do, that such destiny was privileged among the nations of the world. Again, many Jews and Christians will well accept the truth of the finite nature of the created order, and still believe that God's providence will somehow prevail. At its most extreme, this view has often inculcated a quiescence toward perceived threats to human well-being on the grounds that God will do something about it. For the most part, however, the Jewish and Christian traditions have been more active, for other doctrinal reasons, in personal and social welfare than in ecological seriousness and concern. The belief in providence, however, is now for many in this tradition difficult if not impossible to maintain. For the Jewish community, this difficulty culminated with the Holocaust, the still unbelievable fact that within vivid living memory around six million Jews were exterminated. It is difficult if not impossible to stand at the gates of Belsen and still believe that God will always intervene to ensure that his creatures come to no harm. Christians are equally affected by this indescribable experience. In the midst of a life in which we once thought that we were all lovingly cared for we have seen the gates of Hell. Moreover, we live in sight of them daily as the news media remain full of stories of atrocity of one sort or another.

The uncertainty inculcated by all this has a profound effect on our general confidence in the moral order of the universe. We can no longer believe in a God who will intervene in our interest, even in the most dire of circumstances. As a result, we know that we are left to our own devices to secure our well-being in a universe which will, seemingly, come to a physical end for no apparent reason at some future date. Though we may still appreciate the marvellous aesthetic beauty of the created order, we cannot lapse into romantic constructions about its innate goodness without massive leaps of faith in the face of so much evidence to the contrary. Suffice it to conclude here that ecological uncertainty in general, and the effect that that alone has had on the traditional Jewish and Christian belief in providence, is a major cause lying behind our sense of ethical uncertainty. We will now conclude this discussion by noting one other such cause: scientific uncertainty.

Modern science, in general, was born out of the simple philosophical observation by Descartes and others, that the beginning of all knowledge is the distinction we need to make between ourselves as knowing subjects and the external world about us. This, to us, unbelievably simple insight had, in fact, been in the making for centuries before Descartes, ever since philosophers such as William of Occam began to insist that knowledge should be based solely on what we can demonstrably know rather than on what some authority teaches that we ought to know. All the sciences as we know them were born in the seventeenth and eighteenth centuries on this then seemingly fully justified confidence in the abilities of our rational powers of observation, experiment and conclusion. Advance after advance followed from this as human beings seemed to conquer the natural order with never-ending success. The high point of confidence in all this came in the mid-nineteenth century and is epitomised by the Great Exhibition of 1851. This was a veritable celebration of science in general and of the pre-eminence in that of the British Empire. This was, moreover, well founded in very real successes as well as the belief that they would continue. And continue, of course, they did, and thankfully still do. Human life benefits immeasurably from the successes of science and nowhere more obviously so than in medicine. More people, in the affluent world at least, now live longer and more active lives than they have ever done in the past. The statistics of all this are well known and staggering. Western societies are now having to re-adjust themselves socially and economically to care for an ever increasing proportion of elderly people. Falling birth-rates in these societies are also, of course, contributing to this.

Even these brief reflections on the benefits science has brought to the human lot are more than enough cause for it to be celebrated. We live, too, with the confident expectation that science will continue to find cures for ills such as AIDS and cancers. But there are clouds in this blue sky which cause concern and uncertainty. Some of our most effective treatments such as those using antibiotics are under threat from the mutation of organisms which have adapted to survive them and are returning to threaten us with renewed vigour. Indeed we have probably, in our innocence, over exposed ourselves to antibiotics and thereby diminished the benefit we can obtain from them. For example, until very recently we saw no danger in feeding them to animals (as aids to livestock management) and then eating the result, thereby exposing ourselves unnecessarily and dangerously to even higher levels of tolerance than is good for our natural immune systems. Such 'eating dangers' as they may be termed are now commonplace. The BSE issue is an obvious further one. All this causes understandable anxiety and uncertainty in individuals and societies. The interface between our scientific knowledge and political judgement is under constant strain and nowhere more so than in the food sciences. Whilst we now know that the methods of science are among the very real triumphs of our civilisation, we know too at a popular and everyday level that they are not as all-conquering as they were until recently thought to be. Behind this now widespread awareness lies a more long-standing question about the limitations of our scientific abilities. We will now briefly consider this.

Whereas we once thought, on the basis of philosophically demonstrable principles, that we could observe the natural order with an objective confidence, we now know that the actual truth of what happens when we make such observations is not so straightforward. In 1932 a German physicist and philosopher, Werner (Karl) Heisenberg won a Nobel Prize for the reformulation of quantum mechanics. Five years before this he published his work on the now famous, 'uncertainty, or indeterminacy, principle', on which this reformulation was based. Contrary to what was then supposed in physics, Heisenberg claimed that it was not possible to determine, at the same time, the position and the momentum of electrons by simple observation. The more accuracy which is sought in the one leads to inaccuracy in the other. The act of locating the electron in the first place requires the use of high levels of light energy and this affects the electron's momentum. In other words, our very act of observation causes the thing, in this case an electron, we are observing to appear to us in different ways. This now accepted fact was extremely controversial in its time because it contradicted the Newtonian derived belief that such things as electrons could be kept under constant observation by which they remained undisturbed. Furthermore, Heisenberg acknowledged that the effects of observation on empirical phenomena could never actually be calculated, with the result that the physical world would ever remain obscure to us. We are left with only probability where we once thought that certainty was available to us. It is salutary for us to remember that at this time philosophers, such as Bertrand Russell, were confidently believing that the physical world was observable to us because the matter of which it was composed was not infinitely divisible. He was so confident of this that, with others, he produced a system of logic based upon it. Needless to say, that too has long fallen into disbelief. It was eventually famously renounced by Russell's philosophical heir and its former chief exponent, A.J. Ayer. The general point that Heisenberg made about the observation of electrons was, he showed, applicable to all such observation of any natural phenomena. As a result, quantum mechanics has again become as much a philosophical subject as it is a straightforwardly scientific one. It seems, moreover, to the unscientific mind at least, to deal with ever smaller and more mysterious entities as it talks of 'prions' and the 'chaos theory' they are part of. Little wonder that all this lies behind our widespread feeling of uncertainty and its bearing on our ethical uncertainty in particular.

In this chapter we have seen why there is every reason to believe that the uncertainty in modern ethics which we examined in chapter 1 is no isolated phenomenon, it is rather itself a manifestation of much deeper and widespread uncertainties which have been centuries in the making and which now reach into all areas of life and thought. It is also important to remember, again, that uncertainty is not always a bad thing: it engenders hope and determination across a range of human activities and, indeed, is probably what has caused human survival more singly than anything else. Human beings have always lived on the edge of their abilities to master their environment, control their diseases and maintain their sanity. This very determination to exist and succeed in the face of uncertainty, whatever it brings, is probably why the species to which we belong has succeeded, thus far, over others who live alongside us in more primitive forms, or who have long since become extinct because of their failure to adapt to the changing and the unexpected. It is probably safe to suggest, however, that uncertainty is now more widespread than it has been in the past, more present in our awareness and more demonstrable in our sciences. For this reason, it puts more strain on our established ways of dealing with the unknown in our religions and moralities. These traditional bastions of comfort and solace are under as much threat from uncertainty as are other areas of life and thought. For this reason they are often abandoned as being irrelevant to the immensity of the task we now face as human beings, as we try to find a basis for facing our uncertain futures.

Our religions, in particular, however, are equally turned to to fill the gaps in our certainties. People who are otherwise sophisticated in their under-standings of life often become eclectic in their attachment to religions, or versions of them, which afford certainty. Scientists, for example, are often as capable of dealing with the obtuse sophistications of their subject as they are of accepting the most fundamental and unexamined claims of religion alongside them. The popularity of fundamentalism in religion in as sophis-ticated a culture as that of North America, is a well known manifestation of this phenomenon. Such anomalies should be avoided if they serve only to prevent us from facing necessary truths about our situation. Nowhere is it more desirable to avoid doing this than it is in morality. We began by seeing why acting morally is the essence of being human. If we get this wrong, therefore, we are betraying something close to our reason for existing at all, and are in danger of not being true to ourselves. For this reason alone, we have to come to terms with uncertainty in life generally and in ethics in particular.

In the next chapter we will examine a number of contemporary writers on Christian ethics who believe that, in spite of all the foregoing, we can nevertheless find certainty in Christian ethics. They do this, as we shall see, in various ways, but they all have in common the belief that there is some-thing about the certain nature of religious knowledge which enables us to counter all other uncertainties. Indeed they invariably commend it for this very reason and, as we have seen, in an uncertain world they are never short of takers. Many of the thinkers we will examine are in influential academic positions and therefore exercise considerable influence. We will see, however, that their certainties are ill-founded and that they offer no real alternative to facing the uncertainty we have identified in other ways.

Chapter Three

SOME CONTEMPORARY ADVOCATES OF ETHICAL CERTAINTY

There are innumerable contemporary writers on ethics who, regardless of anything we have considered so far, still insist that certainty can be achieved in the subject. They are not at all ignorant of the difficulties, far from it, but believe that they can be overcome. Of these, the Christian writers who believe that certainty is attainable in morality fall, broadly, into two groups. These, again broadly, are Protestant and Roman Catholic. The Protestants, as might be expected, base their certainties on the Bible and the Roman Catholic writers also do this in part, but also, as again might be expected, base their ethical certainties on ecclesiology and, in particular, on the role of the Church as the Magisterium; the definitive teacher of the faith. We will consider writers from each of these positions in turn. In what follows it will be shown why these arguments are all unconvincing in different ways and why, also, we need to look elsewhere if we are to come to terms with uncertainty in modern ethics and culture. Later chapters will set out the alternative approach which is not susceptible to the criticisms we will now consider.

The contemporary Protestant writers all more or less work under a single influence, so before we consider examples of them in turn we need to understand a little what that influence is. It is that of Karl Barth (1886–1968) a Swiss–German theologian. He still towers over modern theology and his extensive writings were based on a radically simple idea. This was one which he came to as a result of his experiences as a young pastor in Safenwil on the outbreak of the First World War. Barth had been theologically educated in the Liberal Protestant tradition under Adolf Von Harnack at Göttingen. This, broadly, shared the liberal optimism of the nineteenth century as well as the general belief in the inevitability of progress which was then being made in the sciences and elsewhere. Harnack confidently believed that the tasks of theology and of science were as one. The implication of this was that the more people understood themselves and the world in which they found themselves, the more they would, at the same time, come to understand God. Harnack was keen to counter the role of dogma in theology and replace it with his own liberal and open approach to modern culture. He combined this with a firm belief that we can penetrate back through the centuries to discover the historical Jesus and, thence, interpret Jesus' message for our own time. Such a Jesus is clearly the Son of God and, therefore, a religious genius without equal in world history. There is, of course, much more to Harnack's theology than these brief remarks indicate, but this, in essence, was his teaching. It is still influential for many in its own right.

In his early years as a pastor, Karl Barth worked confidently in this Liberal Protestant tradition, but all that was to change dramatically on the outbreak of the First World War. The scale with which the horror of the war broke on a Europe that had either forgotten the nature of war, or remembered it as only being localised and small-scale can perhaps be better appreciated by us only in retrospect. War was no longer a temporary and localised adventure. It had now become a horror in its own right which produced death and suffering on hitherto unparalleled extents and, even more to the point, for no apparently good reason.

All this was exacerbated for Barth when ninety-three of Germany's leading established intellectuals signed the 'Manifesto of the Intellectuals', a document which endorsed the war in general and the Kaiser's policies in support of it in particular. The younger generation of scholars became horrified by this and most of them reacted in one way or another. In later life Barth vividly recalled his own reaction when he saw Harnack's name on the document along with those of most of the teachers he had formerly admired. 'I suddenly realised', he wrote, 'that I could not any longer follow either their ethics and dogmatics or their understanding of the Bible and of history.'[1] The nineteenth century and all it stood for theologically and ethically had ended in debacle. This was the twilight of the Gods in which theology had to begin again if it was to enable people to come to terms with the war and, above all, to know what to do about it. Theology needed a 'wholly other' foundation which was not compromised by the war. With his fellow pastor Edward Thurneysen, Barth turned to scripture and in particular to St Paul's Epistle to the Romans. Theology, he rediscovered, must begin with God and not with humans. Only in this way can it judge human fallibility and help to redeem a fallen world. Barth's *Commentary on the Epistle to the Romans* was the result of this change of mind and it soon led him away from Safenwil to Tübingen as Professor of Theology. The rest of his extensive writing was all based on this fundamental insight which dialectically juxtaposed the word of God and all human words and, thereby, gave Dialectical Theology, as we now know it, its name. This theology claimed that theological ethics, like all other theology, should be based on revelation. Barth dramatically likened God's gift to humans of moral insight to his gift of the promised land to the Israelites.[2]

This brief recall of the reasons why Karl Barth came to think as he did has been necessary so that we can understand something of the way in which his latter-day followers share his position. We shall see that they too, in various ways, subject modernity to the word of God as it is revealed in scripture. Again following Barth, however, their use of scripture is invariably selective, since they acknowledge with him that it is uneven in the way in which it reveals God's word. For them, the key to its power is its strangeness to us. This is what makes it God's word for us. It is not God's only word but it is the source of our understanding all else that God says to us by other means. This is the influence we shall now see at work in some of the contemporary Christian writings on ethical certainty.

An extremely important modern work on the New Testament seeks to understand what Barth meant when he claimed that ethics should be based entirely on revelation. This is Richard B. Hays's, *The Moral Vision of the New Testament*.[3] We will now look at this book in the light of its broad agreement with Barth, see what conclusions it comes to about the nature of Christian morality and then subject those to brief evaluation. Hays is Professor of New Testament at Duke University Divinity School and an overall commendable characteristic of the text is that it is derived from refined teaching material. This, at once, explains both the thoroughness and the clarity of the book and is the reason why, as we shall see, it stands in its own right as a work of exposition, even if the reader chooses to differ from some or even all of its conclusions. No serious student of the subject should now be without it as a work of reference. The extensive bibliography is a resource in itself. The book is so extensive that we need to gain some, albeit brief, understanding of its content before any initial assessment can make sense.

Whilst not entirely uncritical of Barth, Hays is in essential agreement with his use of scripture and its attempt to formulate a moral theory which is based on the revelation it contains and which remains authoritative for us. Indeed, part of his criticism is that Barth occasionally allows *too much* room for considerations of modernity in his biblical ethics.[4] Hays writes of Barth:

> In a time when the church is enervated by lukewarm indifference and conformity to the surrounding culture, Barth's theology offers it a potent shot of courage. His hermeneutic is comprehensive and radical in its incorporation of the witness of Scripture, though it is not always clear how Barth reasons from Scripture to his particular ethical judgements. In any case, by adopting Barth's hermeneutical perspective, the church can affirm its identity as a people whose vocation is above all obedience to the Word of God.[5]

As we shall see this is also the case with other contemporary writers on Christian morality. Hays's acceptance of Barth's general position could not be clearer.

Hays's hope is not that his 'book will settle all disputes but that it will facilitate a clearer discussion about how to read the New Testament and how to live in imaginative obedience to its moral vision'.[6] This, at once, explains its necessary length. It is divided into four parts, each of which we will need to consider separately.

The Descriptive Task: Visions of the Moral Life in the New Testament

This begins with the writings of St Paul for the reasons that he, of all the New Testament writers, wrestled most extensively with ethical issues and because his are the earliest Christian writings. Paul's ethics are seen to be integral to his theology and to its constant development in ever changing circumstances. We will consider the wider significance of this later. The Pauline ethic is shown to be premised on three 'fundamental warrants' that are intrinsic to his Gospel; that union with Christ causes newness of life, that freedom from sin should inspire allegiance to the one who caused the freedom, and that the work of the Holy Spirit enables living the moral life in the community. As is generally acknowledged, Paul is seen as primarily a preacher and organiser who engages ethical issues as a consequence of his pastoral obligations. The remainder of this section considers developments in the Pauline tradition and each of the Gospels with concluding sections on the question of the historical Jesus and the book of Revelation.

The Synthetic Task: Finding Coherence in the Moral Vision of the New Testament

Having considered the 'individual witnesses' in part 1, this asks how 'these various ancient texts function as a canon'.[7] This is attempted by following three 'procedural guidelines': all the texts have to be confronted, tensions between them have to be allowed to stand, and their literary genre has to be allowed for. Next, Hays argues that coherence can only emerge if 'images' are sought which reflect the 'narrative coherence' of the New Testament, since no single image, such as that of 'love' or of 'liberation' can do the job. The ones he chooses are: Community, Cross and New Creation. These, he claims, 'bring the moral vision of the New Testament canon into focus and provide a matrix within which we can speak meaningfully about the unity of New Testament ethics'.[8]

The Hermeneutical Task: How do Ethicists use Scripture?

How, that is, are the texts of the New Testament actually read as a message addressed to us? Obviously, only a selective answer could possibly be given to this question and the selection Hays chooses is the way the texts are read in the writings of Reinhold Niebuhr, Karl Barth, John Howard Yoder, Stanley Hauerwas and Elisabeth Schussler Fiorenza. These are wisely chosen as being largely representative of different traditions, but they tend numerically, inevitably perhaps, to favour Hays's own preferences. The task is then further narrowed to looking only at what these writers have said about war and violence, with the conclusion that the views of Barth, Yoder and Hauerwas 'most adequately capture the full story adumbrated by these images' (Community, Cross and New Creation). As a result, Niebuhr's neglect of the covenant community and selective use of the New Testament texts are unsatisfactory. Schussler Fiorenza is found wanting because she reads the New Testament only through the focal images of Community and New Creation to the neglect of the Cross.

The Pragmatic Task: Living Under the Word

The issues discussed here are: violence, divorce and remarriage, homosexuality, anti-Judaism and ethnic conflict, and abortion. These are chosen only to represent methodologically how the proposals made in the earlier sections work out in practice. These discussions are followed by helpful and often moving concluding pieces of autobiographical information. It is concluded that 'the New Testament texts call us to respond in imaginative freedom, under the guidance of the Holy Spirit, to form communities that will embody the truth of the Word, demonstrating metaphorically the power of God's grace in our midst.'[9] It is added that this conclusion calls for nothing less than 'a fundamental transformation of the church'.

Such a range of discussion is seldom encompassed in a single volume, which is the main reason why it was pointed out above that its importance stands for the reader whatever view she or he takes of the conclusions arrived at. But what are we to make of these conclusions, in furtherance of Hays's express wish that they should be seen as an aid to an ongoing discussion?

Hays's conclusions are premised upon two assumptions about the ethics of the New Testament: that they can be synthesised into a single coherent message, and that this being possible, that message can become normative for all subsequent Christian moral endeavour. We will examine these assumptions, briefly, in turn.

Even a cursory reading of the New Testament reveals its diversity and nowhere more than when it discusses ethical issues. Divorce is a case in point; Mark forbids it, Matthew allows it on a condition, and St Paul wrestles with the marriages of believers to unbelievers in a way which suggests that, although he is aware of the Markan prohibition, he gives other advice 'I and not the Lord' (1 Cor. 7:12). Hays recognises the difficulty of reducing these different witnesses to a single canon, but believes nevertheless that it is possible to focus on the norm being a lifelong marriage between one man and one woman and by interpreting this through the motifs of Community, Cross and New Creation.[10] He gives numerous other examples of the way in which seeming ethical diversity can be reduced to singular canonical instruction. An alternative view can begin, rather, by accepting the diversity of the New Testament as given and by trying to get behind it to see what was happening in the dynamically unfolding life of the early Christian Church. Given the extent of diversity in the New Testament on ethical, not to mention numerous other issues, this would seem to me to be a way forward which has a greater respect for the New Testament text *as it is*, rather than as we would like it, for whatever reason, to be. Furthermore, by what explanation, other than divine guidance, could some authors who wrote unbeknown to each other possibly be expected to produce the synthesis required? To reply that this is proof of divine intervention, is but to invoke a circular argument and, thereby, to prove nothing. We will return to this question of synthesis after examining Hays's further claims that what is so synthesised becomes normative for all subsequent Christian tradition.

Hays claims that 'The New Testament is fundamentally the *story* of God's redemptive action; thus, the paradigmatic mode has theological primacy, and narrative texts are fundamental resources for normative ethics.'[11] By this he means that in any ethical discussion the New Testament texts 'must be' granted authority.[12] This, of course, immediately raises the question of the authority of extra-canonical texts. He replies that they cannot be used as independent counterbalancing authorities because 'the *Bible's* perspective is privileged, not ours'.[13] The stridency of this conclusion could, of course, only be sustained if the prior assumption that the ethical teaching of the New Testament could be synthesised had been established. We have already given reasons for doubting the possibility of this.

So far we have seen only that Hays's interpretation of the New Testament is open to serious question. It remains to ask whether contemporary Christian ethical endeavour is best served by his view or by some other. To take another poignant example, Hays is clear that the New Testament moral canon enjoins pacifism.[14] The reasons why many and probably the majority of Christians think otherwise are well known and lie behind the Just War theories. These existed before New Testament times but were Christianised by St Augustine and others as Christians faced the need to reconcile their collective responsibilities as citizens with their individual spirituality. Hence the necessary and continuing debate about war and peace outside the pacifist traditions but within the Christian tradition. In all this the New Testament is not ignored, rather the contrary. It is placed in the context of changing needs and circumstances which have arisen since it was written. Other examples could be given of why Christians have faced the need to *continue* the ethical debates of the New Testament rather than simply accept that they ended there. Such examples would include the ethical issues we are now increasingly confronted with as a consequence of our burgeoning technologies.

Finally, is it not the more exciting and ethically the more challenging to understand the pursuit of Christian moral virtue as being as demanding on us as it was on the women and men of New Testament times? Our ethical life, so understood, is not meant merely to be a cipher of theirs, it is, rather to be seen as the continuation of their striving to work out the meaning of their faith, even in fear and trembling. Seen in this way, what we do ethically is, in kind, a continuing part of the ethical life of the New Testament. Our faith, like theirs, is still in the making. It enables us to face modernity just a they did, and we cited the instance of St Paul in 1 Corinthians 7 as just one example of this. There are many other such in the New Testament. When Christian morality is seen in this way it requires us to turn to the New Testament no less earnestly or often than when it is seen as Richard Hays wishes. We look, rather, at *how and why* it comes to the conclusions it does *as well as* to the conclusions themselves. This alternative view generates in our ethical life both immediacy and urgency, not to mention an intimacy with the divine moral imperatives, whatever they might for us turn out to be in any given situation.

To differ in this way with the conclusions of Hays's enquiry is not, as was pointed out above, to detract at all from its quality or its practical usefulness in the ongoing debate. It is but to reply in the spirit he encourages, as we seek together to know what the Lord requires of us in our ethical endeavours and never more so than in our uncertainties which are many and can be expected to remain so this side of the fullness of the Kingdom of God. The Christian faith gives us good reason to hope that things will then be otherwise.

As we have briefly seen there is a consistent resonance in Hays's approach between the conservative way in which he treats the biblical text and the equally conservative ethical conclusions he arrives at; on, for example, pacifism, and divorce and remarriage. The same is true about his approach to homosexuality. He writes on this subject with extreme and poignant sensitivity when talking of a close college friend, Gary, who was HIV positive and who has since died of an AIDS-related illness. Hays is careful to claim that the biblical text should not be used as though it relates directly to and solves our problems, but the conclusions he comes to certainly have the appearance of doing this. He believes that the text prohibits homosexual intercourse and enjoins 'lives of disciplined sexual abstinence'.[15] For this reason, he is opposed to homosexual marriage and approves in principle the ordination of homosexuals providing they are celibate.

Impressive though Hays's scholarly achievement remains, his claim that it is possible to synthesise the moral teaching of the New Testament and use it normatively in whatever situation we find ourselves, consistently claims too much for the text by failing to allow its diversity to stand. It also fails to take seriously the way in which others have used the text, wrestled with the range of ethical problems and come to other conclusions. The conclusion that Hays is reading morality back into the text and not out of it is irresistible. In the end, he turns the biblical text into something it clearly is not, a coherent whole with consistent messages; he imputes those messages with normality and judges modernity in the light of them. The consistently conservative ethical conclusions he comes to, as a result, add up to a very traditional use of the text on the one hand and inflexible approach to modernity on the other. And all this is notwithstanding the erudite scholarship and pastoral sensitivity of the writing. In the next chapter we will see, in more detail, why such a use of the Bible is unacceptable.

Our second example of an influential theological ethicist who writes under the self-confessed influence of Karl Barth is Stanley Hauerwas. In his latest book, *Sanctify Them in the Truth*, he begins by acknowledging his agreement with Barth's claim that ethics in general and the good in particular is addressed to us by God in Christ. Barth writes:

> When we speak of ethics, the term cannot include anything more than this confirmation of the truth of the grace of God as it is addressed to man. If dogmatics, if the doctrine of God, is ethics, this means necessarily and decisively that it is the attestation of divine ethics, the attestation of the good of the command issued to Christ Jesus and fulfilled by him. There can be no question of any other good in addition to this.[16]

There are three related emphases in this claim which Hauerwas approves; that in the Christian tradition ethics, doctrine and human sinfulness are inextricably linked. In this way, goodness is revealed to sinful humans by a righteous God and such revelation is unique in the sense that the knowledge so derived is not available by any other means. 'For Barth,' writes Hauerwas, 'indisputably the greatest Protestant theologian of this century, there can be no ethics that is not from the beginning to the end theological.'[17] In his writings over a period of twenty years Hauerwas has blended this indebtedness to Barth with appreciation for other and even seemingly diverse Christian sources such as the writings of St Thomas Aquinas. An emergent and constant theme is that ethics in the Christian tradition is expressed in narrative forms that are sustained in the Christian community from which they derive their meaning and coherence with a way of life, outside of which they have no meaning. Bible-reading is central to this and it is the Christian community which makes biblical interpretation possible. Living in and studying the history of that community are preconditions of moral virtue. This is what makes discipleship possible through confession, forgiveness and grace.

Hauerwas disavows having any particular ability as a biblical scholar and attributes that to his Liberal Protestant theological upbringing. For this reason he shows his constant indebtedness to Barth and more recently to

John Howard Yoder. Hauerwas uses the biblical text selectively and not systematically, in the sense that it conforms to any previously established principles.

The emphasis on ecclesiology in Hauerwas's writings naturally results in a focus on social ethics, understood as the ethics *of* the community, rather than ethics *in* the wider community, as that term is more usually taken to mean. In his *A Community of Character,* he challenges directly the Liberal Protestant assumption that there is a correlation between Christian values and those of liberal democracies in which virtue can be found. Against this, he asserts that there are what he calls moral limits to secular polity which can only be transcended in and through Christian community. In making this claim he is critical of the writings of Reinhold Niebuhr and others because the enthusiasm they have engendered for Christian social and political engagement has caused the Church to overlook its more profound political obligations which can only be expressed by its challenge to secularity. 'Nowhere', he writes, 'is the effect of this more powerful than in the Christian acquiescence to the liberal assumption that a just polity is possible without the people being just.'[18] The most disastrous consequence of this, he observes, in the life of the Church is that it pursues its virtues by imitating the policies of secular liberalism. Interestingly, a similar and equally powerful protest of this kind was made by Edward Norman in his Reith Lectures of 1978 in which he criticised the churches in general for allowing 'themselves…to define their religious values according to the categories and references provided by the compulsive moralism of contemporary intellectual culture'.[19]

For Hauerwas the Church stands over and against contemporary culture just as the Bible stands over the Church. In this way, the instrument of God's self-revelation is embodied in the life of the faithful where alone it has meaning and whence it challenges a secular world. Throughout his writing Hauerwas refers constantly and often movingly to his indebtedness to his own Methodist Church congregations which have enabled him to articulate and sustain this theology. His latest work is dedicated to one such for this reason. Those at all familiar with Methodist theology will notice appreciatively the way in which Hauerwas, classically, intertwines the pursuit of personal holiness with pastoral care and social action.

Before we evaluate Hauerwas's theological ethics it will be helpful to consider just one area in which they have focused on a particular ethical opinion. It is one in which he unapologetically draws a normative conclusion which he then presses on others. It is that of pacifism. It is reported that he frequently tells his students that he will convert them to it before they finish his course. References to the subject can be found throughout his writings, but his essay entitled 'Pacifism: Some Philosophical Considerations' is perhaps most revealing of his position.

He begins by making it clear that although his pacifism raises interesting philosophical issues it is of theological and not philosophical origin. This means that it does not seek deontological or utilitarian justification as though it needed the status of either. It is, rather, theologically intrinsic in the sense that it arises from the sort of life Christians are enjoined to live because they have been given the Gospel. For this reason it is an affirmation, rather than the prohibition it is, in his view, often mistaken for. 'Rather,' he writes, 'pacifism follows from our understanding of God which we believe has been most decisively revealed in the cross of Jesus Christ.'[20] In obedience to the Cross, believers, he claims, are called into a community that is governed by peace. The community is their mandate for behaving as they do. It will already be clear how resonant this particular position is with Hauerwas's general theological ethics, briefly considered above. He defends the view against the most common objection; namely, that it is contrary to the Christian obligation to love and protect one's neighbours. Surely, this objection runs, love does require that we protect others, especially the weak and otherwise vulnerable, by coming to their aid forcefully if there is no other way of doing so. Not so, replies Hauerwas, for the simple reason that the attacker in any such situation has equal claim to our love. 'The attacker, who may well be unjust, is no less an object of God's love than the one being attacked.'[21] If this results in tragic consequences, then, he adds, they are no worse than those which would have resulted from forceful intervention in the first place. To live in this way is to participate in the divine being, to live the sort of life God lives and hasten his kingdom as no alternative course of action is able to do. In particular, he identifies the Christian just war tradition as failing in this respect, that is, it does not respect the obligation to love the aggressor. In further criticism of that tradition, he rejects the legitimacy of any state which enjoins its citizenry to take up arms. Such a state even if it is a democratic one 'must surely deserve to be described as the beast'.[22] Against such a state, the pacifist witness of Christianity is the only hope, the only embodiment of God's love which behaves as God does Godself. Having now considered Hauerwas's theological ethics in general and this strident example of their application, we are in a position to evaluate them.

Hauerwas is as clear an example of the espousal of certainty in the face of uncertainty as can be found among contemporary writers on Christian ethics. He does not deny, of course, that we face uncertainty. He leaves that to the wisdom of God and enjoins only that we follow that wisdom as it is revealed to us in Christ Jesus. All else is impiety; all rational calculation, all compassion requiring forceful action and all belief that we must perchance risk the compromise of our own piety in the service of others.

Stanley Hauerwas writes well and engagingly for a wide and appreciative audience. Moreover, as we have briefly had good reason to observe, he also exemplifies a particular sort of nonconformist Christian spirituality which is admirable in its consistency and often courageous in the face of evidences to the contrary. Theologians do not generally achieve such consistent reconciliation of biblical theology, ethics, doctrine and spirituality in a single compass. Yet, it must be asked for our purpose, does even all this support the certainty it espouses?

Note, first of all, that in Hauerwas's view, no matter what topic is under discussion, modernity is always subordinated to the biblical text and the ecclesiology it supports. The thought that as we discover ever more about the mysterious world in which we live we might have to change our views of the Bible and Christian tradition is never entertained even as a possibility. Mainstream Christianity has had to make a number of shifts of opinion in the light of its ever-developing secular knowledge. There are innumerable examples of this: its view of the age of the world in the light of evolution, its view of the unacceptability of slavery in the light of the development of liberal democracies and concepts of human rights and its view of the equality of the sexes in the light of the rise of feminism, to mention only three. Yet another is the difference that our understanding of sexual orientation as not being a matter of free choice is having, in part, on the now widespread Christian reappraisal of homosexual relationships. In all these instances, the Bible and tradition have had to be and are being revisited, not abandoned, in the light of these important pieces of empirical information. Hauerwas, or the general position he espouses, would not allow the legitimacy of rethinking of this kind. Moreover that position implies that not only has nothing already happened to cause us to rethink our interpretation of the Bible and Christian tradition on this topic or others, but that nothing could possibly *ever* happen to cause us to do so. This is, frankly, incredible. Its imperviousness to modernity devalues all human endeavour and culture to an unacceptable degree. Whatever things human beings might have done wrong, and there are plenty of them, they also have much to their credit as the most successful of the planet's species. A theology, such as that of Hauerwas, which does not recognise this must be judged accordingly.

Hauerwas and the Barthians in general write of the Bible and Christ as though both were untainted by culture. This, again, is really quite incredible. The Bible, as we shall see in the next chapter, is in large part a profoundly multicultural document which reflects on its every page the cultural milieu out of which it came and against which alone it can be understood. The Christ is also a cultural figure, a literary construction erected to interpret the historical Jesus. It is possible that there are some forty titles of Jesus in the New Testament alone, each one of which is taken from elsewhere and applied to Jesus. In a classic study of this subject Oscar Cullman writes: 'The reason for his [Jesus] being described in so many different ways is that no one of these titles by itself can comprehend all the aspects of his person and work. Each of them shows only one particular aspect of the whole wealth of convictions of faith about him which we find in the New Testament.'[23] All these titles were cultural constructs which originally applied to persons and concepts other than Jesus. The only title which he is shown as applying to himself, incidentally, is the 'Son of man'. As we have already mentioned in passing, the extent to which the influence of Barth's theology has encouraged such a-cultural thinking about biblical and Christian origins is worthy of a study in its own right. This shared position can be found among theologians who are opposed to one another on important other issues.

Finally, if we take Hauerwas's pacifism as a paradigm of his thinking about ethics, what are we to make of it? It, again, has the advantage of lucidity and coherence, but does it really help us to overcome the usual objections which are marshalled against the pacifist positions in general? Do we really think, in all conscience, that if an evil assailant is about to harm an innocent child that that assailant deserves our *equal* consideration *in every respect*? And more: if such an assailant was about to afflict innumerable such children, would we still think the same? Radical evil is, for whatever reason, an ugly fact of the world in which we live. Can we really stand at the gates of Auschwitz and do nothing? These brief comments will show why I am as convinced that I can convince my students of the truth of non-pacifism as Hauerwas is of convincing them of his position! Not of course that my position solves the problem. On the contrary, there is an immense amount of effort which always has to be expended in working out the details of the Just War alternative to a pacifist position such as that of Hauerwas.

More generally, as we shall see in later chapters, the Bible and Christian tradition have always been the subject of revision and reinterpretation.

There is no such thing as a 'Grand Narrative' which comes to us unscathed through the centuries from some time when it was revealed to us intact and never again to be changed. Some, indeed probably the far greater majority, of Muslims might interpret the Qur'an in this way, thereby making their religion truly a religion of the book; but that has never been the case in the mainstream Christian interpretation of either the Old Testament or its own writings in the New. Again, we will see in the next chapter that even the biblical text itself is better understood as containing the dynamic of a changing narrative rather than a grand and unchanging one for all time.

For these reasons alone, albeit with reluctance, we cannot accept Stanley Hauerwas's sophisticated interpretation of Christian certainties as a bulwark behind which we can stand to reject uncertainty in modern culture and ethics. We will now turn to examine yet another attempt to establish such certainty against uncertainty. This time it is one by a writer in the UK, Oliver O'Donovan, who we shall see also draws heavily on Karl Barth's emphasis on the centrality of revelation in morality.

O'Donovan defines morality as 'man's participation in the created order'.[24] Christian morality is the response of humans to God's act of self-revelation in Jesus Christ. This makes that response a participation in the divine life. But, he rightly asks, how can we be sure of such divine wisdom when our knowledge is limited to and by the created order whence we derive it? This is, in fact, one of the central questions of theology. Interestingly, it provided a controversy in nineteenth-century English theology which, in its time, commanded more attention than the contemporaneous controversy generated by Darwinianism. On the one hand, F.D. Maurice claimed that our knowledge of God was a knowledge of God as God actually is. Against this, H. Mansel countered that such a knowledge was not a knowledge of God in its entirety, but only a knowledge which was sufficient for our salvation. Indeed, most theological agendas throughout the ages contain this debate in some such form. For O'Donovan such knowledge of things as we have must, in his words, 'relate to the totality of things'.[25] He immediately qualifies this by adding that it is not, of course, the sort of knowledge God has, but it does enable us to grasp what he calls the 'shape' of the whole which is acquired from the human point of view. To this he adds 'the exercise of such knowledge is tied-up with the faithful performance of man's task in the world, and that his knowledge will stand or fall with his worship of God and his obedience to the moral law'.[26] In all this, the authority of Christ is central. It is an authority conferred by God, located in the public realm and it triumphs over death. In this way, O'Donovan links resurrection with the moral order, hence the title of his major work which states emphatically that 'Christian ethics depends on the resurrection of Jesus Christ from the dead'.[27] As a result, the moral task is that of describing the moral authority of Christ. This has three features, it is: irreplaceable, good news, and historical. All this means that, 'Jesus' moral authority is evangelical in the fullest sense, since the moral order he proclaims is the kingdom of God, the theme of his message of salvation.'[28]

The form of the moral life which results from all this is, according to O'Donovan, designated by love. He is aware, however, that this conclusion could end just here, in coded rhetoric. Many Christians, in fact, do just this in the belief that they are guided to loving acts by the power of the Spirit. At its most extreme, such a view holds that when moral acts are understood in this way, they need no further justification. There are, of course, all too many tragic examples of such a view ending in tears and death and even mass suicide. Religious moralities which do not account for themselves beyond such limits are no less perverse than secular ones which enjoin blind adherence to vacuous principles. O'Donovan is well aware of this and is careful to point out that the moral life is made up of innumerable acts of human agency rather than of one response to a single principle.[29] Each of these presents an opportunity for moral learning.[30] But, how, according to O'Donovan, does this take place? How does he understand the transition from his theological ethics which we have been considering to the inescapable minutiae of detail that is part of every moral decision however trivial it might seemingly be? Neighbourliness is central to his answer to this question. We are to love our neighbours as ourselves individually and collectively. The two loves of God and neighbour are one love and all other commands are subordinate to it.

At precisely this point we begin to search hard in O'Donovan's writing for some clear explanation of how he translates the foregoing theological rhetoric, excellent though it is, into act, the sort of act demanded by each and every ethical decision. Actual moral decisions, he tells us, are pure simplicity and they owe nothing to the otiose complexities of skill, insight or successful performance.[31] Everything we do morally as human beings, in the end, either does or does not constitute a response to God's love. We will now briefly consider, by way of example, how this relates to just one ethical problem; the question of the rightness or otherwise of remarriage after divorce.

Following St Paul, O'Donovan believes that there is a God-givenness about the single and the married states of existence and that there is no halfway house or compromise between them.[32] Each must be carefully chosen if it is to become the vocation which it is, thereby enabling sin to be avoided. Of the two, marriage must be the most carefully chosen because there is an obvious presumption for the single state and because in the teaching of Jesus, in the Kingdom of God marriage is transcended. At this point, O'Donovan recognises that a dichotomy exists between the Christian ideal of marriage and what a society is likely to accept for it in its legislation. His preference is to stay close to the ideal, but in recognising the validity of the socially acceptable argument he is, clearly, letting into consideration an issue other than those he has defined as being alone acceptable in the canon of his theological ethics. Just this one example gives us the central clue to the way in which O'Donovan wants to preserve certainty in his theological ethics. It is by thus staying close to the confessional root of his ethic as the God-given ideal and by judging as less than ideal such things as the compromises made in divorce laws by a secular society. Certainty is contained in the revealed, and for him this means the biblical tradition and it is a given which is not compromised by qualification or deviation. All the latter is part of the stuff of a fallen world which can only be redeemed by responding to God's revealed love as vindicated in the resurrection of Jesus Christ.

The question we must obviously ask is: is the price O'Donovan pays for certainty in his theological ethics too high? Are we really prepared to preserve the integrity of the ethic and the certainty that it thereby affords by keeping it untainted by the world in the rigorous manner he insists upon? Even some biblical writers themselves were not prepared to do this. In divorce, for example, Matthew allows an exception to the hardness of inflexible rule and St Paul does likewise in affording a privilege. And, this is the point, both of these biblical writers did this because they were reacting to perceived pastoral needs. In other words, these biblical writers were reacting to problems concerning marriage and divorce in a way which O'Donovan thinks is unbiblical! Now, I am of course aware that he would no doubt ably defend himself against this charge, but it docs raise fundamental questions about the way in which the Bible is used in a confessional ethic of the sort O' Donovan advocates. We will return to this issue in the next chapter. It will be necessary to do so if for no other reason than because the three writers we have so far considered in this chapter as advocates of certainty in morality all appeal to the Bible in similar ways.

O'Donovan's writing on Christian morality and the central place he gives to a certainty which is derived from revelation and resurrection is impressive but does it add up to a full account of what such a theological ethic needs to be? We will argue, as we have been doing, that it does not. The fundamental reason for this is that it fails to incorporate as fully as it should the place of redemption and salvation in a Christian theological ethic, discuss the topic though he repeatedly does. For him there can be none of these things unless the fallen world turns away from its wickedness and responds to the purity of a revealed higher order of things. But, is the world really like this? Is it really so bad in essence that it is not redeemable as it is, however imperfect that redemption might be and has to remain this side of the kingdom of God? Are we really prepared to pay the price of a counsel of perfection for the ethical certainty we seek? Are there not lesser perfections in a fallen and uncertain world which are sufficient for our salvation at least? The Church has invariably and thankfully thought so. Even amid the confusions of our morality, there must be other ways of availing ourselves of God's redeeming grace.

The three foregoing writers all, in their own related ways, attempt to seek certainty in the Bible. For this purpose they place it over and against the world in which the certainty is so sought rather in a manner which has been typical of reformed theology as it has followed Luther and others who set the precedent for using the Bible in this way. These writers have combined this with their dialectical and other theological understandings in what, regardless of our view, must stand as sophisticated attempts to find ethical certainty. In the next chapter we will see why the use of the Bible in this way is unacceptable, as well as considering an alternative way of relating it to our ethical endeavours. Before we do that, however, we will consider one other major way in which certainty has recently been sought in Christian morality: not so much, directly, through the use of the Bible, but through ecclesiology; through understanding the role of the Church in such a way that *it* becomes the agency of ethical certainty. There is, of course, nothing particularly new in this since this is precisely how the Church has always been seen by many. What is perhaps new is a marked return to older emphases of this kind and a turning away, by the Roman Catholic Church in particular, from more open and accommodating understandings of the relationship of the Church to the world and its role within it. Such a reaction against 'the world' is one designed precisely for the purpose of finding theological and ethical certainty. So, is it any more successful than the three attempts to do this which we have already considered and found wanting?

Finding certainty within ecclesial boundaries is, of course, as common among the Protestant sects as it is a feature of Roman Catholicism. Many of these sects reinforce the certainty they find in the Bible with the authority of their own traditions. This makes many of them inflexible and exclusive often to the point of sheer arrogance. As a result, they often exercise considerable and, even at times, total coercive power and authority over their members. For this reason they invariably appeal to those who are un-self-confident and they, in turn, can often become exploited in one way or another. The vulnerabilities of the young are, of course, a constant concern in this area. Collective religious certainty is sadly amenable to often despotic control and exploitation, but it is seemingly so desired by enough people for the sectarian form of Christianity to maintain a perennial appeal to significant numbers. More generally, groups of believers who coexist alongside and within mainstream denominations also often display sectarian-type certainties in religion and morality. The most widespread of these in recent years has been the so-called 'charismatic' movement. Its sheer vigour has provided no small part of its appeal to 'ordinary' believers who want more from their religion than alternatives seem to provide. In this movement many of them have found a sense of belonging and certainty in doctrine and morality that the mainstream churches to which most of them continue to belong often seem unable to provide and this has often, in itself, been enough to cause unease between the movement and those churches. In this way, closed certainties have often come into collision with more open and reconciling attitudes and become the source of at least potential division.

We will now consider what is, by far, the most impressive contemporary and wide-reaching attempt to provide ecclesial certainty in religion in general and morality in particular: that found in the encyclicals of Pope John Paul II. He defined an encyclical as:

> a document in the form of a letter sent by the Pope to the Bishops of the entire world: 'encyclical' means circular. It is a very ancient form of ecclesiastical correspondence that characteristically denotes the communion of faith and charity that exists among the various 'Churches', that is among the various communities that make up the Church.[33]

He issued twelve of them between 1979 and 1995, and they cover a breathtaking range of subjects, in an attempt to formulate the meaning of the Christian faith in the light of the many questions about contemporary life and thought which Christians and others are asking. These encyclicals will stand as one of the very great achievements of the present pontificate marking its incredible intellectual energy and determination to address the concerns of the faithful and maintain their allegiance. We will consider just one of these because it focuses on the topic we are considering; the way in which ecclesiology is used to provide certainty in religion and morality. This is *Veritatis Splendor* which was issued on 6th August 1993. The very title, of course, displays a magnificent self-confidence in the face of uncertainty: 'The Splendour of Truth'. The reader is left in no doubt whatsoever about what to expect and, as we shall see, is not confounded.

The Encyclical attempts to define the general principles upon which the Church bases its teaching. For this reason, it does not treat in great detail the minutiae of conduct on specific issues, since this was done immediately previously in the *Catechism of the Catholic Church*, published in 1992. *Veritatis Splendor* is consciously and deliberately a pronouncement on morality for the new millennium which is made necessary because of widespread uncertainty in the subject. This uncertainty, it argues, arises from excesses of human freedom which are brought about by 'a tendency to grant to the individual conscience the prerogative of independently determining the criteria of good and evil and then acting accordingly'.[34] All this results, it is concluded, in an individualism which denies the truth of others and this in turn denies also the 'very idea of human nature'. It may be observed that the Encyclical is best understood as being part of a wider and sustained attempt by this Pope to restore the position of the Roman Catholic Church to its traditional role as the custodian of collective virtue and arbiter of conscience. If this is so, then it is also part of an attempt to redefine the role of the Roman Catholic Church as it was understood in the Second Vatican Council and by many of its own moral theologians who are now working under that influence. Indeed, something like this must be the case if we are to understand a little of the obvious tension which frequently exists between John Paul's pontificate and Roman Catholic moral theologians, many of whom have as a consequence been prohibited from teaching and writing as official Roman Catholic theologians. Before we proceed further with understanding *Veritatis Splendor* it will help if we first try to understand why this has happened.

The issue concerns the relationship of the Roman Catholic Church to secular culture in general and, in particular, to the way in which it considers the significance of the givenness of ordinary human experience. The Second Vatican Council showed itself, surprisingly to some and welcomely to others, very willing not only to listen to this experience, but also to recognise that it is a legitimate source of divine revelation and, therefore, of moral wisdom. In the document *Gaudium et Spes*, on the 'Pastoral Constitution of the Church in the Modern World', the contemporary human condition is analysed in a way which willingly recognises both its obvious achievements and its moral good faith. By this means it is valued as a part of the unfolding of the divine plan for creation. 'Thus,' it concluded, 'far from thinking that the works produced by man's own talent and energy are in opposition to God's power, and that the rational creature exists as a kind of rival to the Creator, Christians are convinced that the triumphs of the human race are a sign of God's greatness and the flowering of His own mysterious design.'[35] In passages such as this the Council not only showed a remarkable openness to human culture and achievement, it also accepted that its recognition by the Roman Catholic Church was a precondition of defining that Church's role in moral teaching. The consequences of all this were immediate and widespread. Roman Catholic moral theologians responsibly made, and still do make, every good use of the hitherto not so obvious freedom to treat the human condition in this way. Examples of this are too numerous to cite and will be well known to many. What they all have in common is a markedly pastoral and reconciling disposition in areas which were more traditionally marked by judgement, albeit compassionate judgement, alone. Little wonder that this general mood raised expectations about the imminence of the change of official Roman Catholic attitude to such things as the legitimacy of using artificial means of contraception. Expectations, of course, which were not fulfilled. However, as we have mentioned, the Second Vatican Council paved the way for the rewriting of Roman Catholic moral theology, and that in turn paved another way for establishing wider collaboration and agreement between Roman Catholic moral theologians and their colleagues in other churches. The undoubtedly beneficial results of all this can be seen writ large in the modern Roman Catholic literature on Christian ethics and morality. In this, insight into contemporary moral issues is repeatedly brought to bear in fresh and constructive ways, thereby bringing that tradition to the notice and benefit of the wider moral community.

The question, of course, for the Pope and his advisors when they prepared *Veritatis Splendor* concerned whether or not the clear direction and even liberties of *Gaudium et Spes* were to be further encouraged. We shall now see that they were not, in spite of the fact that the Encyclical protests (too much?) its general agreement with the Council. Paragraph 29.3 goes explicitly out of its way to confirm this, but this is followed in 29.4 with the assertion that because of the Council's teaching, 'there have developed *certain interpretations of Christian morality which are not consistent with "sound teaching"* ' (actual italics).[36] It continues immediately by stating its understanding of the duties of the Magisterium in the face of this; it must show why 'some trends of theological thinking and certain philosophical affirmations are incompatible with revealed truth'. It is, therefore, impossible not to come to the conclusion that throughout the Encyclical there is a repeated attempt to redress the Council's conclusions and, what were for many, encouragements. After further exploration of this we will then consider the implications of that for our purpose of asking whether or not the ethical certainties and the way they are offered in *Veritatis Splendor* are acceptable.

The subject of the Encyclical is a bold and repeated one: where is virtue to be found? It opens with the parable of the Rich Young Ruler and interprets it in a way that makes it clear that the path of virtue is a costly one. The ruler's question is the same as that asked by every individual: what must *I* do to be saved?[37] And the answer is the same; only by forsaking all others and turning to Christ will this be possible. This poignantly sets the scene for the main theme of the Encyclical: the reaffirmation of the supreme role of the Magisterium in ethical teaching and the precondition it makes for its acceptance; that of forsaking all others. After a mild disclaimer, the role of the Magisterium is boldly stated, 'in order to "reverently preserve and faithfully expound" the word of God, the Magisterium has the duty to state that some trends of theological thinking and certain philosophical affirmations are incompatible with revealed truth'.[38] All these trends, according to the Encyclical have one origin; they derive from an over-emphasis on human freedom and, as a result, deny the transcendent.[39] 'Certain moral theologians',[40] the document continues, have denied Roman Catholic doctrine, by acknowledging this freedom as a source of divine inspiration and thereby denied that there is in 'divine revelation, a specific and determined moral content, universally valid and permanent'.[41] From this the Encyclical bluntly states, 'No one can fail to see that such an interpretation of the autonomy of human reason involves positions incompatible with Catholic teaching.'[42] The diagnosis of the problem and the identification of the nature of its cause could not be plainer.

Against all this, the Encyclical argues that the Church must assert its defence of 'universal and unchanging moral norms'.[43] It is the job of the Church to teach these norms with a compassion which is not be deterred when it is accused of 'intolerable intransigence' in the face of human need.[44] Those who oppose the Church by drawing attention to the acuteness of human need in this way are identified as new Pharisees, because they fail to eliminate from their morality an awareness of their own limits and sin.[45] The barb here against 'the Moral Theologians' could not be sharper; theologians, that is, who have in their own and various ways empathised with the complexities of the human condition on the one hand and related them to the teaching of the Roman Catholic Church on the other. Many of those who have done this in the recent past have brought the teaching of the Church to bear on ethical problems with a new freshness and insight and thereby brought its abiding value to the attention of many who would otherwise have rejected it. This is not to be. The task of teaching revealed truth in morality is to be the task of the whole Church, including the moral theologians.[46] Theology, including moral theology, is 'an ecclesial science'[47] which can only take place in the community of faith as it is defined by the Church's Magisterium.[48] As a result, moral theologians are to co-operate with the Church's Magisterium by setting 'forth the Church's teaching and to give, in the exercise of their ministry, the example of loyal assent, both internal and external, to the Magisterium's teaching in areas of both dogma and morality'.[49] Such theologians are enjoined to accept and remain faithful to the teaching of the Church, something which they cannot do if they oppose it in any way.[50] Dissent '*is opposed to ecclesial communion and to a correct understanding of the hierarchical constitution of the people of God*' (actual italics).[51]

It would be difficult to imagine a more strident defence than this of the assertion that uncertainty in modern morality can be countered with ecclesial certainty. *Veritatis Splendor* asserts that there is only one way to moral truth and certainty; its way. Hierarchical pronouncement is to prevail over all opinion to the contrary, even and especially that within its own ranks, as well as any backed by the force of democratic protest of one sort or another. As we have briefly seen, and as any familiar with the nature of moral debate within the Roman Catholic tradition in recent years will know, there has been plenty of effective opposition to it of both these kinds, encouraged, no doubt, as we also briefly saw, by the teaching of the Second Vatican Council with its vision of reconciling the teaching of the Church with the profundities and challenges of ordinary human experiences. Phrases such as this latter, of course, clinically hide their deep importance in a world where Roman Catholic moral teaching on human reproduction (to mention only one topic) has to come to terms with the unimaginable human burdens of over-population and the AIDS epidemic. Against all this and in spite of hope of a change to the contrary, the Roman Catholic Church has maintained its opposition to the use of artificial means of contraception, even as a way of preventing the spread of the HIV virus through sexual intercourse in sub-Saharan African and other countries where it is rife and public awareness of what to do about it is at a minimum. By contrast, there is evidence that devout Roman Catholics in more educated societies exercise their own freedom of judgement whilst, at the same time, ostensibly at least, maintaining their orthodoxy. Without demonstration, the Encyclical castigates its own moral theologians as epitomising the exponents of the absolute freedom in morality which it attacks throughout. At the very least, this does them a serious injustice, since so many of them write in ways which are as much in opposition to such absolute freedom as the Encyclical itself.

For many Christians this clarion-call to reinstate the *status quo ante* in Roman Catholic moral theology will be a welcome one. Many, however, will not welcome it but will not, at the same time, openly protest against it, since there is no such culture of explicit protest in that tradition. The maligned moral theologians who are often also devout priests and compassionate pastors will either persist in their wider quest and have to face the consequences of disapproval, or they will subtly go about their business in other ways to avoid attention and controversy and patiently await a change in the official position which they hope will become more congenial to their views. Priests close to the everyday agonies and spirituality of ordinary people, will react in their own ways, many of which will be sympathetic to beliefs and practices not approved by the Magisterium. All this marks a return to a position in Roman Catholic thought and polity which many outside that tradition had hoped was a thing of the past as that tradition came to play its important part in making common cause with other Christians and people of goodwill in finding redress for the world's ills.

For the position stridently outlined in *Veritatis Splendor* to provide certainty in morality, at least two things would have to be the case and both can be demonstrated as not being so.

The first is that it would have to be established beyond any reasonable doubt that the Magisterium is always right. Throughout *Veritatis Splendor* there are modest asides about what the Magisterium can actually achieve, but these are unconvincing and never lead to any discussion about the fundamental assumption of inerrancy which pervades the document. A central question which it does not address is: how does the Magisterium itself arrive at the truth? It implies that it possesses it and that for all purposes of discussion, that is that. It does claim to be guided by the Spirit and makes much use of scripture, but eschews the significance of human history and experience, such as that expressed in natural law thinking which has traditionally played such an important role in Roman Catholic moral thinking. Interestingly, it gives more prominence to biblical quotation and reference than is usual in such writings.

The second thing which would have to be the case for the position of the Encyclical to be defensible is that it would have to be shown that it is impossible to believe that God ever communicates Godself through ordinary human experience and affairs. At the very least this, at once, wipes out innumerable biblical traditions which claim that human affairs both individually and collectively are an arena in which the knowledge of God is to be found. Even more pointedly, the position of *Veritatis Splendor* effectively denies the possibility of human beings obtaining any knowledge of God or of virtue through other Christian denominations and other religions. There is only one source of doctrine and knowledge of moral virtue; that of the Magisterium of one Christian Church.

All this is a massive attempt to change the direction of Roman Catholic moral thinking as it has developed since and under the encouragement of the Second Vatican Council. Few external observers believe that it will succeed in this aim in the long term, arrest that thrust though it may well do for the time being. All we need note here, for our purpose, is that *Veritatas Splendor* has not made a case for achieving ecclesial certainty in morality, not even among the religious community for which it was intended to achieve that very thing. The point made here is not that *Veritatas Splendor* failed because it used bad arguments. It failed because, in spite of its ambition and sophistication, there simply are no better arguments it could have used. The central argument is plainly unsustainable. As we will see later, there is an important place for ecclesiology in morality, but this is not it. It simply claims too much and aspires to a certainty based on nothing other than the weight of its own authority. This authority, moreover, was and still is being challenged by the very thing it tries to deny; a wider openness to our understanding of truth and virtue in which it has a part to play, but not the uniquely definitive one it claims.

Other such attempts to counter modern uncertainty in morality with certainty from within the Christian tradition could be examined, but we have considered three such by non-Roman Catholic writers and one major Roman Catholic Encyclical as attempts to achieve this and found them all wanting. The prices they ask us to pay for achieving certainty are too high. They demand that we sacrifice too much of our intellectual grasp of the way the world now is and they leave us with even more questions than they purport to solve. From this we conclude that, however else we might come to cope with uncertainty in modern morality from within the Christian tradition, we can neither deny its existence nor pretend that it can be countered by certainties such as those which these contemporary advocates are putting forward.

This conclusion need not deter us from our continued expectation that the Christian tradition can yet come to our aid, because it does contain insights into and proffers the means which will enable us to live with uncertainty in modern ethics. The remaining chapters will show why this is the case. Why, that is, a religion like Christianity is able to cope with ethical uncertainty by enabling us to live with this uncertainty, thereby neither denying its existence nor by pretending that we can counter it with certainty where none exists.

Before we examine this alternative Christian approach there is one obvious question we will have to consider. It is this: how can we use the Bible in Christian life generally and in morality in particular? All the above attempts to establish certainty, including the Roman Catholic one, rely heavily or exclusively on the Bible. Moreover, no Christian morality could call itself such unless it showed how it understood the Bible, since eschewing it totally is clearly not an option. Neither need it be desired. In the next chapter we will address this question and see how, by using the yield of our critical knowledge of the Bible, we can come to understand its important place in our moral thought and aspirations. When we have done this we will see how, freed from the encumbrance of mistaken, though popular and widespread, views about the Bible we are able to understand just how Christianity enables us to live with uncertainty in modern ethics.

Chapter Four

THE BIBLE AND ETHICAL
UNCERTAINTY

The central argument of this book is that a Christian ethic helps us to cope with uncertainty in modern ethics, though not for the reasons commonly supposed by the writers we considered in the last chapter and others who believe that Christianity and the Christian ethic has more to do with certainty than it does with uncertainty. As we also saw in the last chapter, most of those who want to appeal to Christianity for their certainties invariably turn to the Bible for the source of them. Since the Bible must remain central to any Christian ethic, if it is to be called such, we must therefore first ask questions about the manner of its proper use.

The Bible we must first recall, spans up to some two thousand years of human history if we count the time between the ancient oral traditions, reaching back into the nomadic campfires of Israel's history, which long pre-dated the appearance of its first literature in about the ninth century BCE and the latest books of the New Testament which date from the second century CE. This is why the Bible is so compendious as well as why it is of extensive historical, cultural and literary diversity. All understanding of the Bible must begin with recognition of these fundamental facts. Unless we do this, the biblical writers will never be able to speak to us for themselves.

We will see why these basic facts about the Bible are extremely important for our purpose. Moreover, by dint of the further impact of Western culture on world history generally, the Bible's influence has been all-pervasive ever since the invention of the printing press made it widely available. This may now be changing, for whatever reason it is now frequently and properly remarked that for probably the first time in the history of recent Western culture the Bible is not at all widely studied, with the result that there is a growing ignorance of its nature and all-pervading influence in common areas of life and literature. Indeed, for this reason it is now not infrequently necessary to give basic introductory talks on the Bible at undergraduate and similar levels where only recently such knowledge could be taken for granted. In general, therefore, we either disregard the Bible out of ignorance, assume too much for it by supposing it to contain the answers to everything, or assume too little for it, by supposing it to contain no truth at all. We will now see why all these views are mistaken and why 'the truth about the Bible is rather more complex and surely more interesting.

We are interested, of course, primarily in whether or not the Bible can help us to cope with uncertainty in modern ethics. For this reason we might reasonably suppose that all we have to do with it, therefore, is to look up what it says about ethics and ignore the rest. We cannot do this for the simple reason that what the Bible says about ethics is not so easily separable from what it says about everything else. In fact, it is scarcely separable at all. What it says about ethics is interwoven at all levels with what it says about everything else.

Nor can we serve our purpose by simply looking at the New Testament and ignoring the Hebrew Bible, the Christian Old Testament. They too cannot be separated, since without a knowledge of the Old Testament we can hardly begin to understand the New and, in addition, there are insights in the Old which stand in their own right. There are no such short-cuts in biblical study. So, where do we begin once we have remembered these preliminary but important points?

First, we have to approach the Bible critically by bringing to bear the best of our scholarly techniques and knowledge of the cultures out of which the biblical texts came. This does not mean that we are thereby and subsequently precluded from approaching the Bible spiritually, but it does mean that we need to have this scholarly priority if we are to enable the Bible to speak to us for what it is and not for what it is not. The story of modern biblical criticism is an interesting one in its own right and is coterminous with the development of modern literary criticism in general. It has now been some two centuries in the making, since in the eighteenth century H.S Reimarus, G.E. Lessing and others began to develop the principles of literary criticism. Indeed, most of them were developed for the purposes of biblical study before they were applied to secular literature. Lessing famously dismissed the claims of Christianity on the ground that 'the accidental truths of history can never become the proof of necessary truths of reason', but his work on primary biblical texts became so definitive that biblical scholars could not ignore it. The first thing Lessing's work established was that the texts were extremely diverse in their literary make-up as well as in the perceived purposes that they were originally written to serve, not to mention the diverse further purposes to which they were put by those who read them. These were the simple but profound beginnings of modern biblical studies and they still stand though, of course, they have been developed.[1] The story of all this has been well and often told and need not detain us beyond noting these outlines. That development continues, as successive generations of scholars hone new methods to correct and build on the old. Most recently, some biblical scholars have been moving away from the older historical/critical modes of reading the Bible in several ways including that of emphasising its narrative nature and exploring the interaction of that with the reaction of the reader as the text is engaged.[2] We will see something of all this as we proceed.

In general, biblical study now lets each of the literary traditions of the Bible, and the individual books which make them up, stand for themselves, at least in the first instance. For this reason, the books must first be set, to the best of our knowledge, in their historical context. Their literary genres must also be studied in order to understand the sources on which their writers drew and the allusions they made. More recently, it has been pointed out that we need to understand the way in which the authors redacted the material of their sources so that we can get some clearer insight into the precise purposes for which they wrote. Yet more recently, as mentioned, we have been encouraged not to forget the overall narrative force of the biblical texts, as perhaps a necessary corrective to subjecting them to relentless minute scholarly analysis. Notwithstanding this, however, the plain truth is that although we might well claim a better insight into all this than our predecessors, we still have a long way to go. This is why, of course, biblical study is such a rewarding activity whether it is undertaken for its own right, or as it is here, for a wider purpose.

In starting as we are with a critical understanding of the biblical text, we are thereby rejecting a fundamentalist approach to it. Biblical fundamentalism is itself a complex but widespread phenomenon. In general, it affords the biblical text the status of a uniqueness which it ascribes to the fact that its writers, though human, were under constraint of divine inspiration. Extreme forms of fundamentalism then take this inspirational meaning of the texts at its face value, whatever that might be thought to be at any particular time. Other forms of conservative treatment of the biblical texts share some of these presuppositions but are more sophisticated. They often allow the validity of critical methods and are thoroughly scholarly in their application of them, but the underlying assumption that the biblical texts are different from any others persists and they are therefore given a special status which, in turn, influences the manner of their interpretation in conservative ways. Therefore, no matter what is being discussed, the biblical texts remain above all else and, in particular, above modernity of any kind. In all their diversity, biblical fundamentalism and conservatism more generally, both fail to recognise that the biblical texts share literary form and often content with secular ones and that, because they are created by human beings, they reflect human shortcomings just as surely as they reflect anything else. Fundamentalism, moreover, usually treats the whole of the biblical text in this way. Selection and rejection is not allowed. Its message is: 'take it all or leave it all'. The first and most obvious difficulty with this is that we cannot possibly take it all because some of it clearly offends our moral sensibilities, and a great deal of it is self-contradictory as well as obscure.

More to the point, the biblical writers themselves did not take everything which had been written previously as being binding for all time and everywhere. They went on being creative and selective just as writers prior to them had done. Furthermore, there is a fine line between what is in the Bible and what is not. The reason why we have the New Testament in the form we do is simply that the Christian Church found it necessary, from towards the end of the second century, to be definitive about the corpus in order to preclude heresy from inclusion within it. In doing this, however, it left out much other Christian literature, including Gospels and Epistles, which was contemporaneous with what it did include. All this rules out a fundamentalist approach to the biblical text and encourages us to look for an alternative way of understanding its real and abiding worth. That way, as we have seen, is the critical way. This does not criticise the biblical text for the sake of it. It does so only in order to clear the way for an understanding of its lasting spiritual value in general and, for our purpose, to understand the help it can give us in the face of modern ethical uncertainty.

In the rest of this chapter we will look briefly at the way the ethical life features in the Old and the New Testaments. Space will limit us to examples only, but they will be chosen as being typical of the wider whole as well as because in their different ways they are central to it. What we will be trying to do is to get something of the 'feel' of the way in which faith and ethics interact in the biblical texts. In this we will see that, contrary to what is commonly supposed, a great deal of uncertainty features throughout. Most mportantly for our purpose, we will see that Jesus is a far stranger figure han we might have thought and that he did not legislate on the ethical life n any detail at all. What he, in fact, did was something more fundamental to t which enables his followers to work things out for themselves, and this is he important point, to do so amid uncertainty.

All biblical writers in their various ways make it clear explicitly or mplicitly that one of the things they are writing about is how people hould behave. The reason for this is a simple one. Religion in Israel was understood to be built on a covenant relationship with Yahweh which bestowed both privilege and obligation. The privilege was that of being 'Yahweh's chosen people' and the obligation was that of doing Yahweh's will, understood as a condition of the continuation of election and covenant. The moral life in Israel was generally commended because it brought the reward of Yahweh's favour and not because it had worth in any ends of its own. Yahweh was not just the only God, Yahweh was also a righteous God who punished wickedness with wrath. For these simple reasons, Jewish religion became distinctive not only for its monotheism but also for its *ethical* monotheism. This was the central message of the great Prophets of the eighth century BCE. It is epitomised in the immortal words of one of them: Amos. His point was that Yahweh was so displeased with the moral laxity of Israel that Yahweh was prepared to exercise wrath o the nth degree so that, at most, only a remnant would be left in Israel. All this was stressed against the then prevailing belief in Israel that covenant meant privilege without obligation, or at least without obligation in anything other than cultic observance. Amos thundered: thus says Yahweh,

> I hate, I despise your festivals,
> and I take no delight in your solemn assemblies,
> Even though you offer me your burnt offerings and grain offerings,
> I will not accept them;
> and the well-being offerings of your fatted animals
> I will not look upon.
> Take away from me the noise of your songs;
> I will not listen to the melody of your harps,
> But let justice roll down like waters,
> and righteousness like an everflowing stream.[3]

Amos spends more time telling Israel what justice is not, rather than what it s, preferring the nation to sort that out for itself. He did stress, however, that it was no personal matter alone. It also had to apply in detail to the political economic, social and military life of the nation.

The writings of the eighth-century-BCE prophets in Israel all resonat with this theme. Only by sincere repentance for transgressions, and ethica ones chief among them, could Israel be saved. The fact is, of course, that i did not work. Historically soon after, Jerusalem fell to Babylonian armies in 586 BCE. Israel's privilege had come to an abrupt end. The price it had to pay for its transgression could not be greater; the loss not only of national identity but also of the superiority that had previously pertained over th other nations. From the ninth century BCE to the sixth, Israel had been engaged in a remarkable social, military and literary achievement. It effec tively re-wrote world history as seen from its own perspective generally and in so doing, secured its superior place among the surrounding nations, a well as its tenure of the Fertile Crescent to which it claimed it had a right a the chosen people. The devastation of exile meant that all this would have t be achieved over again if the religious claims made by Israel in its own favour were ever to be taken seriously in the future.

The Prophetic witness was maintained in all this by Jeremiah to whom the then king of Israel, Zedekiah, turned for support when it looked a though all was about to be lost. 'Is there any word from the Lord?' he aske in desperation. To this Jeremiah famously replied: 'You shall be handed ove to the King of Babylon' (Jer. 37:17). After this happened Jeremiah sustaine his prophetic work by giving advice to the exiles who were weeping by th rivers of Babylon. 'Build houses and live in them' (Jer. 29:5), and above a accept 'a new covenant with the house of Israel' (Jer. 31:31). Only this coul lead to a new spiritual beginning and perhaps only then to the restoration c Israel's wider fortunes.

This brief discussion of ethical monotheism in Israel, of the failure of th nation to observe its tenets and of the role of the Prophets in it all, has mad some important points for our purpose of understanding the nature of th ethical life in the Old Testament. First and most importantly, the ethical li is seen as being inseparable from the religious one, with the result that i failure meant not only religious but also political, economic and militar collapse. In all this, the details of what the ethical life requires in every situ ation and for all time are not set out. They require, rather, constan reflection and reinterpretation as is exemplified in the Rabbinic tradition Moral dangers are frequently warned against, particularly when they offen common justice, but what is proffered positively is not at all codified or se out in any detail. Rather, a right spirit is commended and the people c

Israel are left to work out what that might or might not require of them and the nation in any given circumstance. Uncertainties abounded in all this. According to Jeremiah, as we have briefly seen, they had to be accepted and lived with. Only a deeply-held right spirit of the heart could ever bring improvement.

Notice, in particular, that in these ways the ethics of the Old Testament is not seen as something expressing codified certainty. The Prophets called for religious repentance as a condition of morality rather than for the following of a particular sort of ethical life as such. What Yahweh wanted or did not want in any given situation could only be clear in outline. It was up to individuals and the nation to work out what it meant in detail; and they seemingly got it wrong.

There are two other important forms of literature in the Old Testament in which the ethical life is to the fore. The first is in the Mosaic commandments and the second in the so-called Wisdom literature. We will consider each in turn.

The Decalogue, or Ten Commandments, features in the Old Testament as the law given by Yahweh to Moses on Mount Sinai. It is mentioned twice in the text; in the book of Exodus chapter 20, verses 2–17 and the book of Deuteronomy chapter 5, verses 6–21. The variations between these two accounts are only slight. Their general tone is negative and they serve only as guidelines to life in the broadest sense. What they require is not in itself unique to Israel since the surrounding nations all had codes of conduct of their own which made similar requirements. They are, however, probably unique as a collection as well as in the way in which they are required to be observed as a matter of national obligation. It has recently been pointed out that they are, surprisingly and unacceptably we might think, addressed to free men, the men who ran Israel, and they say nothing about the obligations of women, children and slaves.[4] Though the commandments had the status of divine origin, they functioned in Israel more as general instruction derived from practical wisdom than as a Law Code as such. John Barton, again, thinks that the origin of the Commandments can be traced back through their alleged divine origin on Mount Sinai to the practical wisdom which was, as we shall see, so much a feature of Israel's ethical life. He adds that they were commended for the purpose of achieving divine favour rather than as ends in themselves.

Even these brief remarks reveal that the Commandments were more likely to be understood in Israel as guidelines than apodeictic divine law: guidelines which had stood the test of centuries of accumulated wisdom rather than as something that burst from Mount Sinai into an unsuspecting world which previously knew nothing of such wisdom. The two narrative traditions in which they appear are, therefore, more concerned to give sanctity to what previously existed and, thereby, to encourage its observance, than they are with dramatic new revelations as such.

All this is a far cry from the popular picture of Moses as some former-day example of the character portrayed by the actor Charlton Heston descending from the mountain. Here is a society which, by dint of its practical wisdom, was trying to find the right thing to do, not only because it sincerely believed that Yahweh had revealed it, but also and more importantly because, by trial and experiment in the face of uncertainty, the society found these things to stand the test of time. Understood in this way, the Commandments do not stand over and against the Wisdom literature of the Old Testament, which we will consider below, they are more profoundly to be understood as a part of it. The fact that they were treated as general guidelines only might generally be deduced from the fact that in much of its life Israel seemed to ignore them. Sexual morality is a case in point here. The pages of the Old Testament show a surprising degree of accepting liberality in sexual attitudes and practices which seem to be unrestrained by any such prohibiting law whatsoever. Guidelines there may well have been and, whilst respect for them remained, the actual stuff of life was lived out in but loose proximity to them, for better or worse.

Passing reference has already been made to the importance of accumulated experiential wisdom in Israel's ethical life. If we are careful to look for it, we can see its all-pervasive presence even in areas, such as the one we considered above, where we would least expect it. In large parts of the text of the Old Testament, however, it is so explicit that these can be designated as Wisdom literature. This has long been recognised, but the extent to which it is the case has only been realised quite recently. More of the literature of the Old Testament is Wisdom literature than was previously thought to be the case.

The principal Wisdom books of the Old Testament are: Proverbs, Ecclesiastes, Job, The Song of Solomon, large parts of Genesis including the Joseph saga, and some whole Psalms, such as 1, 49, 78, 127, as well as couplets in others. The Apocrypha, is of course largely made up of Wisdom literature. Wisdom, so understood, is not revealed by God to humans in any historically interventionist sense. It is derived from human experience over long periods of trial and error in which success is valued beyond all else and that, in turn, is interpreted to be of the will of God. It is what has been described as 'a quite elementary form of the mastering of life'.[5] It is anthropocentric rather than theocentric, of extremely ancient origin and found in all the cultures of the ancient Near East. It is expressed in pithy sayings and couplets which can be transmitted verbally, and easily recalled when needed to serve as guidelines in any given situation. Naturally, it is at home in cultures which respect age and experience above youth and inexperience. The practical issues the literature addresses are endless. For example: law and order (Prov. 4:14–17), land possession (Prov. 22:28), the poor and the causes of poverty (throughout), idleness (Prov. 12:11), ignorance (Prov. 13:18) and wine drinking (Prov. 23:20–1); to mention only a few. From even this brief list of examples we can see how down-to-earth and practical the concerns of Wisdom actually were. No area of human life is too trivial or controversial to be included.

What the Wisdom literature does not do is lay down prescriptively and for all time what everyone should do in every possible situation. What it does do, is to make available the wealth of accumulated experience as a guide and for reference. It does, further, enjoin people to respect it, but whether they do or not is seemingly up to them. They must work that out for themselves as through their own experience they put the wisdom to the test and, in so doing, confirm or reject it in an ever-developing and accumulating tradition. In all this, there is a marked openness to the past as well as to the future, but the focus is on the here and now, on the verification of what wisdom teaches in the living experience of the acting individual striving to find her or his place in wider society. The criterion for its acceptance is, blatantly, success; whatever works. We will take this point up again in the final chapter.

Understood in this way, the morality of the Wisdom literature is open and dynamic rather than closed and static. It leaves the individual free to work things out for her- or himself. The wisdom of the past is always there, but it is never exclusively binding for the simple reason that it was itself discovered by trial and error, the continuation of which is vital to the living and accumulating insights into morality in the Wisdom traditions. It needs to be asked, of course, in what is now described as the 'reception history' of the Old Testament, why this open and dynamic approach to morality is not considered as typical of it as the legalistic ones. It might even be for a reason as simple as the fact that the phrase 'Thou shalt' has a memorable resonance not only in the text itself, but also in the uses to which it has been put in Jewish and Christian literature, art and liturgy. Whatever the answers, as we have seen, we have continuing biblical critical studies to thank for the fact that we are now more aware than we ever have been of the all-pervasive nature of the Wisdom approach to life and morality in Israel. Its continued study is imperative.

We now come to the question of the Law in Israel and of its place in the ethical life. We do so just before we turn to an examination of the ethical life in the New Testament because, as we shall see, the relationship between that and the Law is a crucial one. This is a somewhat vexed subject for simple linguistic reasons. Our word 'law' does only scant justice to the range of material in the Old Testament to which we apply it. The Ten Commandments, for example, are not referred to as law at all. In the books of Exodus and Deuteronomy they are called 'word'. The reason for keeping the Law in the Old Testament is the same as the reason it gives for heeding wisdom; so that happiness, security and prosperity can be achieved. There is no distinction here between what is sacred and what is secular. All life is covered by the Law and, for that reason, can be brought into harmony with the divine will. The function of the Law is, therefore, an enabling and an educative one. It was not, for that reason, thought of as being prohibitive or restraining in any way. On the contrary, it was liberating to the point of being a source of delight and constant celebration, a thing to be accepted willingly and positively. And so it remains for Jewish believers generally. It is difficult for those who, for whatever reason, see law as restraint to under-stand this. Difficult to the point of not enabling us to see what a life of liberty the life of the Law was and remains. It was also a life of blessed assurance that the divine will was being observed. The keepers of the Law have changed their identity throughout Israel's history, but they have always been seen as pastoral figures and keepers of wisdom as the Rabbis are to this day.

This brief insight into the nature of law in the Old Testament should, again, be enough for us to hesitate before we conclude that the ethical life was only one of prohibition and restraint. Overall, that life can be seen as something quite to the contrary. It was open, innovative, respected the freedom of its devotees, anticipated the future and, above all, it was positive and liberating. There is clearly far more here for us to learn to our benefit that we might have supposed, as we seek all these things in the circum-stances of our own lives. We will discuss the abiding significance of this later after we have considered its continuities and discontinuities with the nature of the ethical life in the New Testament.

The New Testament is made up, broadly, of two types of literature Gospels and Epistles. They all come out of the extremely diverse and rapidly changing life of the early Christian Church over a period of some hundred years or so. As would be expected for this reason, they contain dissimilarities as well as similarities and they all occupy their own distinctive places in the literary history of their times. All this makes for a subject of study which is interesting in its own right, let alone for the important light it throws on our knowledge of Christian origins. In what follows we will thread our way briefly through all this for one purpose: that of getting some 'feel' for the nature of the ethical life as it was therein generally understood. Again, we will see that it is a life which is characterised by openness and freedom more than it is by anything else. And again, we will see why understanding it in this way is important for our purpose: that of discovering how Christian morality helps us to cope with modern ethical uncertainty.

In one way and another all the New Testament documents focus on the person of Jesus. We, therefore, need to ask of them: what can we actually know about what Jesus said and did; how was that understood by those who wrote about him; and how was that, in turn, understood in the rapidly evolving life of the earliest Christian communities? We will begin this daunting task by looking at the Gospels.

There are four of them. Three are similar in both their literary form and in the synopsis or general view they take of the life of Jesus. For this reason they are called the Synoptic Gospels. They are, in the generally agreed order of their appearance: Mark, Matthew and Luke. For all their similarities, however, they contain important differences. These arise from the obvious facts that they were written for different groups of Christians at different times when different needs were paramount and different understandings of what the Gospel required prevailed. We will have to keep all this in mind as we proceed. John's Gospel is different from them. First, in the sense that the historical picture presented of Jesus cannot be reconciled with that presented in the Synoptics. Second, in the sense that the context in which the Gospel was written was also different. Here is a closed community set apart from the world, whereas the Synoptics throughout are redolent with worldly interaction of one sort and another.

In what follows, we will consider how each of these gospel writers understood the nature of the moral life as a prelude to extracting from that, in as far as we are able, an overall view of that life in the teaching and example of Jesus. Even after that, we will have to consider the way in which all this was received in the Early Church and, particularly, in the writings of Paul and the later New Testament writers. Only then will we be in a position to summarise the nature of the moral life as it is understood in the New

Testament before we turn, in chapter 5, to discussing its relevance to our wider purpose.

All four Gospels are unique in their literary form. They are made up largely of short couplets which pre-existed orally in the earliest Christian communities, as well as possibly in previously existing short collections. We do not even know for sure why the Gospels were written at all, since there is only one explicit allusion to such purpose in the book of John chapter 20, verse 31, 'these [things] are written so that you may come to believe that Jesus is the Messiah, the Son of God, and that through believing you may have life in his name.' Luke, as we shall see below, gives a more general reason for writing as he does. We do know that the gospel writers were selective in what they chose to include in their works and that they felt at liberty to arrange in whatever order best suited their purposes. Indeed, we can learn quite a lot about those purposes by studying the way in which they individually edited, or redacted, the material at their disposal.

In all probability, Mark's Gospel was the first to be written, in Rome and/or for Christians in Rome who were suffering the Neronian persecutions in 64 CE. In turn, both Matthew and Luke had access to Mark though they both used it in different ways. Matthew is the most Jewish of the Gospels and Luke the most Gentile. The latter is probably the last of the three Synoptics to be written and is possibly as late as the early second century. All this is the stuff of ongoing scholarly debate but the outline here given is the generally accepted one. All the gospel writers saw the moral life as an inextricable part of the life of faith and, in so doing, echo the same general theme we saw to be the case in the Old Testament. We will now consider how each of them did this.

Mark, it may seem strange for us to realise, is not that interested in the moral life as such for the simple reason that he believed that the world was soon to come to an end (Mark 13). The Neronian persecutions were the presage of that and throughout he encourages his readers to follow Jesus by enduring suffering as he did (e.g. Mark 13:8). The ethics it enjoins is one of a discipleship in which Christians draw together against the persecuting world. It is largely a negative one. The most important thing is that they must not do anything which will jeopardise their imminent chances of salvation. 'Watch' and 'wait' are the keywords. In the meantime, self-denial and endurance are all. The certainty with which the end is here expected in itself explains why Mark shows little interest in legislating for the ongoing Christian ethical life.

Matthew essentially follows Mark, but, appearing as this Gospel did some twenty or so years later, it comes as no surprise to us to discover that it contains the clear belief that, although the end is still expected, it will be delayed, (Matt. 25:1–13). For this reason, Matthew is forced to pay more attention than Mark to the ordinary concerns of everyday life in which Christians had to make decisions, ethical ones chief among them. The Gospel enjoins righteousness as the key to morality (Matt. 5:20). It is the reason given for Jesus' baptism by John (Matt. 3:15). It is also given as the reason why the Pharisees fail in their morality. Matthew's morality is one of a strict inner purity which comes from having a right relationship to God (Matt. 5:20). Love, for Matthew, as defined in the Great Commandment, is what enables all this to be translated into the stuff of everyday life (Matt. 22:38). Matthew is even more explicit than Mark in giving a desire to enter the Kingdom of Heaven as the reason for doing the right thing (Matt. 5:45). In Matthew chapter 5, verses 21–48, Jesus is portrayed as working with Jewish legal traditions, but doing so in a way which makes them all much looser and, undoubtedly, more difficult. Obscure though many of these sayings are and undesirable though it obviously is to take them literally, they do show an understanding of a Jesus who wrestles with and adapts central traditions.

Luke's Gospel is different again. Unlike the other two Synoptics, it has a sequel: the Acts of the Apostles, and this is the key to understanding its difference. Luke tells us that he sets out to tell the whole story of Christianity from the beginning to when St Paul preaches the Gospel in Rome openly and unhindered (Acts 28:31). A further difference is that Luke is resigned to the indefinite delay of the coming of Jesus which is why he is at pains to explain the present work of the ascended Christ. Little wonder that it is in Luke, for the first time in the Synoptic Gospels, that we encounter anything like a clear concern for the nature of the not only ongoing, but also seemingly indefinite, ethical life. That the Gospel does not do it to a greater degree than it does is an indication of just how difficult the Early Church found it to accept the fact that the world had not come to an end. Luke is clearly resigned to the indefinite nature of history, but does not go on to work out the implications of that for the Christian ethical life in anything other than an introductory way. In fact, he adds little in this respect to the previous gospel writers. It was left to others to achieve this as the circumstances of the life of the Church changed, particularly after the conversion of Constantine and after that, the fall of Rome. We will see in what follows that this work still continues.

The Gospel of John and the Epistles, like the Synoptics in their related and separate ways, have their own approach to the ethical life. It focuses on the new commandment. 'I give to you a new commandment, that you love one another. Just as I have loved you' (John 13:34). 'One another' here is central to the Johannine view of morality. It is premised on the life of faith, a life which requires the rejection of all worldly concerns, one which can only be fulfilled by living in the community of faith. So understood, the Christian moral life is one of renunciation and of turning inwards. Only in this way can sanctification be found. We cannot be sure about whether or not, or if so to what extent, the Johannine circle of faith was an open one.[6] In all probability, the Johannine Churches would have differed in their practice, but the main thrust is a clear one. The moral life has to do with renunciation. Only in that way can unnecessary conflict be avoided and the requirements of the life of faith lived out to the full. The Church, so understood, might well proclaim the Gospel *to* the world and thereby invite it to join the circle of the faithful, what it does not do is to consider itself responsible in any way *for* working out the world's salvation as such. It certainly does not concern itself with worldly behaviour outside its boundaries. In these ways, the Johannine writers clearly and consciously set out, in their view, to correct the understanding of the Church found in the Synoptics. The biblical scholar and theologian Rudolf Bultmann puts this succinctly, in saying that, 'it is ultimately a transformation of the Church's understanding of itself'.[7] Here is a church which quite deliberately and self-consciously sets out to transcend the world and thereby to make its members strangers within it. Here is a life set apart: a life of devotion to the community of the Church, with but scant regard for the welfare of what lies beyond, other than trying to include it within its boundaries. The New Testament contains all the archetypes of ecclesial arrangement which were to work themselves out in Christian history and this is clearly one of them. We will discuss below the place of love in the Christian moral life.

The Gospels are the 'filters' through which we have to try and discern the life of Jesus and reconstruct his teaching. As we have briefly seen, they are all written from distinctive, if in parts related, points of view and these clearly act as controls on what is or is not included as well as on how things are expressed and the priority given to them. Much nineteenth and twentieth-century New Testament scholarship has been preoccupied with the extent to which we can, or cannot, reconstruct the life of Jesus from the Gospels. For our purposes we must now ask whether or not we can reach back through the traditions to obtain some understanding of what Jesus said about ethics. We have glimpsed how the gospel writers did that, but what does their writing add up to? And is it anything that we can make use of in our understanding of the ethical life? What follows is a brief attempt to answer these fundamental questions.

The New Testament might well contain different ways of relating the life of faith to the ethical life, but it is consistent in its insistence that they are inseparable. Faith and ethics are one. There can be no life of faith which does not have ethical implications and there can be no ethics without faith. This much is resonantly clear. Indeed, the nature of the ethical life is indicative of the acceptability, or otherwise, of the life of faith and vice versa. They stand or fall together. This is clearly one of the fundamental ways in which the understanding of the ethical life in the Old Testament is taken up in the New. This is why it is possible to talk of a Jewish and Christian morality. Diverse in its expression thought it may be, it remains consistent on this theme and it is one to which we will return in later chapters, where we will explore what it means to understand the ways in which the life of faith and the ethical life share vulnerabilities in the face of uncertainty.

All the gospel writers mention the place of love in the teaching of Jesus and the Christian ethical life, but they do so in surprisingly different ways which are important for us to recognise. As we try to do this, it is salutary to remember that our 'view' of *the* Gospel is invariably a mental amalgam which we put together from them all, a bit from here and a bit from there. For the most part we get by with this, but it often stands in the way of our seeing more profound meaning in the Gospels which only gives itself up to us at all if we keep their differences, as well as their similarities, in mind.

When Matthew's Jesus was asked by a Pharisee what was the greatest commandment of all (Matt. 22:36, paralleled in Mark 12:28–34 where the same question is asked by a Scribe), he replied, 'You shall love the Lord your God with all your heart, and with all your soul, and with all your mind. This is the greatest and first commandment. And the second is like it, You shall love your neighbour as yourself.' In this way, Jesus is clearly stating what it means to be faithfully Jewish. Here, again, the Old Testament and the New are at one. The first part of his reply is a quotation from the book of Deuteronomy chapter 6, verse 4ff., and the second part is a further quotation from the book of Leviticus chapter 19, verse 18. Both quotations were prominent in Jewish liturgies, just as they were to become in Christian ones. Here is the great summary of the Law, the distillation of everything else it says. Again, we will later explore the implications of this radically simplified ethic for our purpose. For now, we need to examine a little further how love actually features in the teaching of Jesus as it is portrayed in the Gospels. The New Commandment is found in Mark chapter 12, verses 28–34 but it is not made a great deal of, beyond serving to point out that the religious authorities were condemned by their own code and not by anything new or radical Jesus had said himself. Mark does not record Jesus as enjoining his disciples to exercise love as such. Indeed, it has rightly been pointed out that if Mark was the only Gospel in the New Testament canon: 'it would be very difficult to make a case for love as a major motif in Christian ethics'.[8] In the rest of the Gospel of Matthew, apart from the repeated mention of love in the Great Commandment (Matt. 22:37ff.), the word is only used once as a moral virtue in the injunction to love one's enemies (Matt. 5:44). There is clearly less said about love in this Gospel than we might at first think, important though the existing mentions are. The same, we shall see, is true of the other Synoptic Gospels. In Luke's Gospel love is only commended, as such, in three passages. In the first (Luke 6:27ff.) it is part of a series of woes and is commended as requiring unlimited benevolence. In the second (Luke 7:36ff.) a sinner's love is forgiven because her love is great. The third (Luke 10:25ff.) is Luke's recording of the Great Commandment. Significant though these passages are, they, like those in Mark, are scarcely enough from which to claim that Luke saw love as the, or even a, central motif. Moreover, the word does not appear at all in the Acts of the Apostles, which is surprising, given the prominence it has in the Gospels even if that is lower than at first sight we might have expected. However, the fact that all the writers preferred the word *agape* to the alternatives, *eros* or *philea*, clearly suggests that they at least shared a general meaning, even if that remains opaque to us.

We have now briefly seen that the writers of the Gospels give different emphases to the place of love in the teaching of Jesus and noted that, even overall, they do not add up to anything like the stress that popular imagination ascribes to them. We will later see that St Paul does not at all give it prominence of place in his understanding of Jesus' morality, though he does think it important in a wider sense. What is apparent from all this is that Jesus is consistently portrayed as being reluctant to be prescriptive about what love requires in particular situations. He seems, rather, to make a point of saying that people must work that out for themselves and we will see that this is arguably the essential key to his teaching on morality. Love itself, is, of course, not prescriptive. It can mean lots of things and Christians, like others, have often disagreed and indeed still do over its exact requirements. From the fact that the Gospels are reasonably clear in their agreement over this refusal of Jesus, we might reasonably (tentative though it is to suggest such) assume that there is authenticity at this crucial point. If so, then we can understand why love is such an important part of the spiritual life, why it is an inspiration to action and why it sustains often heroic moral endeavour. And all this remains in spite of the fact that love is not in itself prescriptive. Indeed, once we are clear about what love is not, we can become the more clear both about what it actually is and what it can and cannot do.

Can we, then, extract from the Gospels an account of Jesus' ethical teaching? This question, of course, begs a far greater one about whether we can find our way back through the Gospels to the historical Jesus at all? Let alone, that is, to just one aspect of his teaching. This question has set the agenda of much twentieth-century New Testament scholarship and has given birth to a genre of it called, appropriately, 'Jesus Studies'. Telling this story, even in outline, would be beyond our scope, but it is important for us to note parts of it.

About fifty years ago, under the influence of the views of Rudolf Bultmann, there was a great deal of scepticism about whether or not we could ever know *anything* about the historical Jesus because all we encountered in the Gospels is the 'Christ of Faith'. However, there was a reaction to this so-called 'Bultmannian scepticism' by his own pupils. They accepted his methods, but applied them afresh and came to less negative conclusions. One of these, Gunther Bornkamm, stridently asserted that 'the primitive tradition of Jesus is brim full of history'.[9] The debate continues. The important distinction between the 'Christ of Faith' and the 'Jesus of History' still stands and it is widely recognised that the latter is a somewhat elusive figure.

Again, largely under the influence of Bultmann who was himself following in some ways Schweitzer much earlier in the century, Jesus has been widely regarded as a strange apocalyptic figure whose main message was: 'the Kingdom of God has come near ; repent, and believe in the good news' (Mark 1:15). This view was taken, in turn, as the reason why neither Jesus nor his immediate followers paid much, if any, real attention to the ongoing requirements of the ethical life and we have already seen something of this in the foregoing. This strange apocalyptic picture of Jesus famously entered the public arena, in the UK at least, by his portrayal in Dennis Potter's play 'The Son of Man'. For this and other reasons it came to be a widely accepted one. It was part of a general picture of the New Testament in which Jesus and his immediate followers were seen to be mistaken in their apocalyptic expectations and in which, also, it was left to others, such as St Paul, to put that mistake right. This background, conveniently, explained two things. First, why Jesus did not say more than he apparently did about morality and second, why so much of what he did say is strange to us to the point of being downright impossible to follow. Do we really want to pluck out eyes, for example (Matt. 5:29)? And is thinking about adultery really as sinful as committing it (Matt. 5:28)? On this view the ethic of Jesus was thought to be an 'eschatological ethic', or an 'interim ethic', the relevance of which was largely if not exclusively confined to its own age. Schweitzer, again, was influential in putting forward this view. More recently, scholars, whilst accepting the correctness of this, have challenged the assumption that because the ethic of Jesus was like this, it had no relevance to the present age. They variously argued that, whilst parts of Jesus' ethical teaching was of this sort, it neverthelesss contained much more which remains valid in spite of the fact that the end of the world, obviously, did not occur as Jesus and his immediate followers apparently expected. The New Testament scholar C.H. Dodd generally put forward a view known as 'realised eschatology' which held that, future-oriented though the preaching of Jesus was, it could nevertheless be realised partly in the present this side of the Kingdom. The ethic of Jesus, understood in this light, was also one in which virtue could be partly but never fully realised. This is probably a generally accepted view among contemporary Christian ethicists. Note, however, that it is based on biblical scholarship which spanned the first half of the twentieth century. Since then, that scholarship has moved on and, for our purposes, it is important for us to understand how it has done so and what the significance of that is for our understanding of Jesus' ethical teaching.

In the last two decades or so, New Testament studies have, generally, paid more attention than hitherto to the influence of Jewishness on the texts, especially the Gospels. In doing so, they have pointed to the fact that their sources, settings and meanings are bound up in large measure with Jewish ones. This is now widely acknowledged and is the simple reason why New Testament scholarship is noticeably more abundant in its reference to Jewish matters than it was even immediately previously. The story of this is, again, fully told elsewhere and need not detain us beyond this mention. We will continue by looking at its implications for our understanding of Jesus' teaching about morality. For convenience we will choose just two recent examples of this, which give different points of view. The first, which we can briefly mention, is Gerd Ludemann's *The Great Deception* and the second is one which has been and continues to be extremely influential in Jesus studies: J.D. Crossan's *The Historical Jesus, the Life of a Mediterranean Jewish Peasant*.[10]

Ludemann promises a major re-appraisal of what Jesus really said and did and has given some indication of what it will contain in a recent publication. His position is a strident one. He writes, 'I...now regard as illegitimate any return to the preaching of Jesus as a foundation for Christian faith.'[11] He rejects the Christian 'explanation' of the cosmos and prefers to accept it as a great mystery. He recognises, as we shall largely do below, that the ethical teaching of Jesus, as such, was developed by others after him and that a human reconstruction of religion is now his (Ludemann's) preferred one. According to him, sayings and actions of Jesus are inauthentic if they: are attributed to the risen Christ; break natural laws; give answers to questions which were only raised after his time; address the concerns of a Gentile audience.[12] On this latter point, Ludemann follows the trend we have already noticed, of locating Jesus firmly back into his Jewish roots. We cannot solve the problems of the text of the New Testament by granting it a special status since, as he rightly points out, that begs the very questions we are trying to answer in the first place. The fact is, he claims, that the sayings and actions of Jesus became heavily overlaid in the earliest Christian communities and that this all happened before the Gospels were written. They simply continued to do the same thing. Ludemann concludes his short essay by claiming that it clears a way to make something more positive possible. As yet he has not essayed what that something will be like.

Ludemann's work has to be noticed for our purpose because it serves as a reminder that we are probably always mistaken when we claim too much for Jesus. We have already seen, in the previous chapter, why it is wrong to claim that the ethical teaching of Jesus gives us easy access to ethical certainty. Here we are left with what we might at most describe as a 'minimalist Jesus' who is a strange Jewish figure, barely intelligible in any of the thought-forms or categories we might use for the purpose of understanding him. This particular debate will continue following the forthcoming publication of Ludemann's more considered thoughts and their fuller treatment, but it has already made the important point: that the Christian Church (and we) claim too much for Jesus too readily at peril of distorting the real contribution he can make to our lives. This is the point well made by Nicholas Peter Harvey that we mentioned in the Introduction. We will follow this up again in the next chapter. In the meantime, we will now look at the second recent work of Jesus scholarship and do so because it accepts the clearly Jewish nature of everything Jesus said and did and is cautious in the claims it makes about what we can understand of it.

The title of J.D. Crossan's book perhaps, as we shall see, says it all. Jesus was a Jewish peasant. Its dust jacket describes it as 'the first comprehensive determination of who Jesus was, what he did, what he said'. Whilst this claim may well lack modesty, it does point us to the potential of the book and prepare us for what to expect. We will now see why this claim is not entirely unjustified.

According to the Bultmannian interpretation of Jesus which, in contrast to the usually short life of scholarly fashions, has held sway for about half a century, everything Jesus said and did must be interpreted within the framework of his work as a prophet announcing the eschaton. All his actions, all his encounters with others, all his sayings, including all his parables, must be interpreted as announcements of the imminence of the end of things as they are and the dawning of the Kingdom of God. Whilst some unease about the stridency of this view has from time to time been expressed, it has generally prevailed.[13] And even those who questioned some of its implications did not so question its basic presuppositions. The result of all this was that a half-century or so of English-speaking New Testament scholarship was in thrall to Bultmann's magisterial achievements. Whilst they still stand and still have much to commend them, particularly to my own generation which was brought up on them, Crossan begins his reconstruction of the life and work of Jesus by challenging them. The historical Jesus, he insists, 'must be understood within contemporary Judaism, [which was] ever more forcibly, a richly creative, diverse and variegated one'.[14] He argues that, contrary to what scholars have on the whole recently believed, it is possible to separate the authentic actions and words of Jesus from the inauthentic ones that exist alongside them in the Gospels.

> My methodology for Jesus research has a triple triadic process: the campaign, the strategy and the tactics, as it were. The first triad involves the reciprocal interplay of a macrocosmic level using cross-cultural and cross-temporal social *anthropology*, a mesocosmic level using Hellenistic or Greco-Roman *history*, and a microcosmic level using the *literature* of specific sayings and doing, stories, anecdotes, confessions, and interpretations concerning Jesus.[15]

All these three levels are equally important at any and the same time meaning that interpretations cannot be premised on any of them to the exclusion of the others. This is a massive scholarly undertaking in its own right and that alone goes some way to explaining the length of the book. Crossan realises that even at this length he cannot be sure to have established objectivity at every point, but he does aspire to what he calls 'attainable honesty'.[16]

The Jesus that emerges from Crossan's discussion is described by the phrase 'a peasant Jewish cynic' and in which the adjectives and the noun are to be given equal weight.[17] The cynicism is displayed by the way Jesus attacked the prevailing mores of Jewish and Roman society; by his manner of 'looking and dressing, eating, living, and relating that announced its contempt for honour and shame for patronage and clientage'.[18] The Kingdom Jesus announced was a 'brokerless' one which cut through every layer and manifestation of self-interest and self-assurance to create 'unmediated physical and spiritual contact with God and unmediated physical and spiritual contact with one another'.[19] In all this, according to Crossan, Jesus did have a vision for civil society, one based on a radical religious and social egalitarianism that negated alike and at once the hierarchical and patronage-based norms of Jewish religion and Roman power. Little wonder, we might add, that it suited the vested interests of both to conspire against him unto death. Here is a Jesus whose attention is very much on the here-and-now rather than on the about-to-be: on the commonplace and ordinary, on the actual circumstances in which people found themselves and on the power of all these normally overlooked things to reveal the will and the love of God. Jesus was, moreover, clear in his reason why people could not see what was blatantly obvious to him. It was their religious, moral and civic pretensions which obscured the truth. The very things, that is, which ostensibly existed to reveal it. Little wonder, again, that the ordinariness of Jesus offended so deeply and that he cultivated it as consciously as he appears to have done. The Gospels frequently mention that he was not recognised for who he was and that he appeared to them as an ordinary traveller or gardener. Indeed, we know that the fact he was so ordinary and not recognised by those who met him for who he actually was, was a problem for the next generation of Christians, at least for those Mark addressed in his Gospel. Jesus, he argued, deliberately concealed his identity from those he met and there is, of course, much scholarly debate about whether or not this claim was an invention of the gospel writer or whether or not it reveals something of the historical Jesus himself.[20]

In the next chapter, we will broadly interpret Jesus' teaching on morality in the light of Crossan's interpretation of his person, life and work. We will then see that this morality was far from directive. On the contrary it was spontaneous, created by challenging rather than by affirming received wisdom, and almost never prescribed anything particular at all. What Jesus did, again and again, to the consternation of all who came to him for advice and direction was to turn questions back to where they came from and to create, in so doing, even greater perplexity. Only when his hearers came to terms with this could they get even close to seeing the real point of it all, which was: that they had to think things out carefully for themselves, from basic first principles and take more notice of the ordinary and the common-place than of their cherished and ingrained assumptions. Little wonder, again, that they and we usually fail. Here was a morality in which there was no place for brokers who derived their authority from received wisdom. There was only the moment, the patently and ordinarily obvious, and, more to the point, the unlettered, the outcast and downright sinners were more likely to get it right than the virtuous. All this, as we will see in the next chapter, is a far cry from what is usually understood by Christian morality. Ecclesiastics and those with all manner of powerful vested interest were subsequently to reclaim this directness for their own, just as those around Jesus repeatedly tried to do, to his consistent disapproval (e.g. Mark 10:35–41). But that is the story of the Church throughout the ages in all its forms. Whilst it always has and still does try to do its best and whilst, also, there could be no surviving Christianity without some such institution-alised arrangements, it remains salutary that the morality of its founder can be interpreted in this way. A way that is indomitable, and resists all and every attempt to institutionalise it. Before we take up these points more fully, however, we need to look briefly at the rest of the New Testament to see how it interpreted the ethical teaching of Jesus. In all this the writings of St Paul are, of course, central.

Even in a brief consideration of Paul's thought, the first question we must ask is: which of the alleged writings of Paul are those we can actually ascribe to him? Arguable though it may be, we will presume that Colossians, Ephesians, 2 Thessalonians, 1 and 2 Timothy and Titus are pseudonymous works which imitate and, in Ephesians for example, considerably develop Paul's thought. They are no less important for this reason and, indeed, might be the more so because of it.

Paul was the first theologian of the Christian Church in the sense that he was the first to think at all systematically about the wider implications of what Jesus said and did. He was also the first ecclesiologist in the sense that he, above everyone else, did so much to found, nurture and build the first Christian communities. For all these reasons, Paul and not Jesus should properly be called the 'Founder of Christianity'. Jesus, of course, made it possible, but for reasons we have briefly seen, he did not found anything.[21] It was probably totally alien to his life and teaching even to think of doing so anyway. His life and ministry ended in the desolation of the crucifixion.

After his resurrection everything was left to his followers, without the success of whose labours all would be lost. What Paul founded was a system of ecclesial organisation, a way of ministering to the pastoral needs of its members, and a way of thinking theologically about those first two things. In this way, Paul was preoccupied with 'the interpenetration of history, theology and ethics'.[22] Paul did not apparently carry out theological reflection for its own sake. Everything he thought was related to the task in hand at that moment; that of caring for the Churches in some predicament or other. He was the archetypal Christian pastor and theologian to whom all who were to come after were to be indebted, whether they knew it or not.

For our purpose we will consider what Paul meant by the 'new righteousness' and why it became so important for the development of Christian morality. Though he developed it in his thought, he did not invent it as such. He took it from sources which were also used by the writer of Matthew's Gospel, particularly in those parts of it which are unique to Matthew.[23] Paul was keen to stress that it was faith which alone brought justification and not the Law (Rom. 9:30–104). He combined this with a radical view of the universality of the Gospel and this was recognised at the Apostolic Council in Jerusalem in 49 CE. In this way, Paul became the champion of Gentile Christianity. This is most stridently essayed in the Epistle to the Galatians where the emphasis is on Christians enjoying a 'new creation' in Christ (Gal. 6:15). This freedom is what righteousness makes possible, simply because of the new relationship with God it bestows. Understood in this way, righteousness is a religious rather than an ethical concept, though it also had a bearing on morality as we shall see.

The new righteousness was nothing less than a new relationship with God.[24] A relationship which had previously not been possible; one which was the opposite of sin and alienation, the ground of a new life in Christ (Gal. 6:15). Nothing the believer has done or can ever do can bring this about. It is the consequence of the free action of God through grace, the only source of salvation. As a Rabbinic convert to Christianity, Paul, like Matthew before him, would naturally be preoccupied with the question about the exact manner of salvation without the Law. That salvation begins with God's free act of redemption in Christ and the believer can access it through faith alone. Nothing else justifies. The righteousness which results is the free gift of God and the manifestation of God's grace in human affairs (Rom. 3:24, 4:4; Gal. 2:21). This alone is what leads to a new life in Christ (1Cor. 12:31) and its power is eternal (Rom. 6:23). Just as there was previously no area of life or thought which lay outside the Law, the new righteousness is also all-pervading. Every area of life and thought is permeated by the life that the new righteousness makes possible (Rom. 8:31–39) and, above all, it is liberating in the extreme. Little wonder that such a strident redefinition of the means and nature of righteousness came to be misunderstood. If there was no sin or any human action at all which it could not redeem it was logical to suppose that the more extensive the sin the greater the grace that abounded (Rom. 3:8). Paul's response to this was to stress that the new freedom brought new obligation. An obligation which existed in the life of the Churches and which was defined, invariably, by himself as an Apostle of the Lord. So defined, the new freedom of faith which was wrought by righteousness was a freedom circumscribed only by the requirements of the life of faith as laid down by his authority. This requires a way of life which was to be exemplary in all things and which stood as an example for others to follow. He understood his own life in this way (1 Cor. 11:1). There was seemingly no length to which Paul would not go to exercise the immense authority all this required and no limit to his impatience when it was ignored.

Although Paul still clearly expects the Lord to return in glory and, indeed, might well have understood his own ministry to be instrumental in bringing it about, his understanding of the moral life is much less affected by that expectation than, as we have seen, it variously was in the Gospels. Indeed, Paul, as we have seen, laid the foundations for a lifestyle which was in the next century to become known as the 'Christian way'. It was by then what made Christianity distinctive, long before that distinctiveness was marked by credal orthodoxies of one sort and another. Whilst he did not work out what this life required in great detail, he did make it possible for others to build on what he had begun. And, this is the point, the Christian Church has been doing that ever since and will go on doing so this side of the Kingdom of God. We will return to this point below.

Paul's ethics were strictly theological for the reasons we have already considered. Although the actual connection between the two in his thought are not at all systematically set out.[25] This view has, however, recently been challenged on the grounds that, although Paul adopts many of his moral norms from prevailing culture, there is nevertheless a coherence between them and his theology.[26] Like the Johannine tradition, Paul believes that love is central to the moral life, but he gives it his own interpretation. Namely: that whoever loves does not do evil to his or her neighbour.[27] Love is the fulfilling of the law (Rom. 13:10), and its genuine acts precipitate the Kingdom in this evil world. It is what he describes as the yet more excellent way in 1 Corinthians chapter 13. A way which encompasses everything that is said and done. Paul did not set this out in anything like systematic form. As the pastor that he was, he addressed specific ethical issues only as and when they arose in the life of the Churches. Here, like the Matthean tradition, he is constrained by a desire to enable people to live in ways which will not prejudice their chances of eternal salvation (1 Cor. 7), as well as by his determination that Christians should avoid anything that might cause schism in the life of the Churches, or scandal of any kind. Above all, however, Paul always shows a willingness to face both actual problems and interpret hard rules in difficult circumstances. The general result of this is that Paul's writing has seemingly uneven tendencies. The emphasis is on whatever is necessary in a given situation, rather than on a carefully crafted and coherent whole. Sometimes freedom is to the fore and at others, such as in the Corinthian correspondence generally, there is more emphasis on rule-making and following. There is no such thing here as a set-piece view of the moral life which is binding on everyone in the same way at all times. Everything is being thought out, so to speak, on-the-hoof, as issues come into and pass out of his daily concerns for the Churches. Of these he founded all those to which he wrote except the Church in Rome. Without the Law, the main task in all this is to understand what the life of freedom requires in any given situation and to carry that out whether it be in sexual, familial, political, or other area of life such as whether or not Christians could divorce their unbelieving spouses.

We are not here concerned to understand Paul's vision of the moral life in detail and for its own sake. For our purpose of getting the feel of morality in the New Testament we need to notice one important point about it. Namely, that it was dynamic, rather than static, and open, rather than closed, to new developments. It oscillated between emphases on freedom on the one hand and obedience on the other, according to the needs of the situation at the time. It is also interesting because whilst still expecting the eschaton, it wrestles with the ongoing nature of life and all that brings in a way that we can still recognise. In so doing, it creates an atmosphere in which the moral life has to be worked out and worked at as a consequence of the life of faith. It is not a thing set in stone. Genuine questions, disagreements, confusions and uncertainties abound, and the more we appreciate them for what they are, the closer we get to feeling the sheer excitement of the life of faith in the Churches to which Paul wrote. Then, as ever since, there was not always agreement about the sort of morality the life of faith required and then, again, those differing either stayed within the folds of particular Churches or broke away from them. Paul, of course, was always at pains to try and prevent this latter from happening and this alone explains the degree of coercion he was prepared to exercise in order to achieve that. All this is a window on a world where the moral life is far from being understood as something set for all time and never to change. It is, rather, something to be wrestled with constantly and must ever be open to new ideas and insights wherever they might come from, including secular sources as well as preceding biblical ones. We will examine all this further in the next chapter. In the conclusion of this one, we will now look briefly at how the moral life is understood in the rest of the New Testament outside the Gospels and the strictly Pauline writings. Again, we will do this only to get the feel of it and to see if here, as in the Gospels and the Pauline writings, the moral life is conceived as something open and dynamic as opposed to closed and static.

Paul's magisterial influence in the emergence of the early Christian Churches was not only important in its own right, it served as an example for others to follow. In doing this they did not simply imitate what he said and did, they also developed it and, in so doing, brought new insights to bear. Noticing this simple point is, of course, important for our purpose. It powerfully illustrates again that the life of faith as it evolved in the pages of the New Testament was no static thing. It was always changing and developing. Not even as magisterial an influence as Paul could prevent this. Those who came after were to 'do their own thing' as he had done his. Imitate him though they might and, following the literary conventions of the time, use his name though they might, they nevertheless went on making the biblical faith in the light of ever new needs and challenges. Those who did this most noticeably were the authors of: Colossians, Ephesians, 2 Thessalonians, 1 and 2 Timothy, Titus and 1 Peter, the so-called 'pseudo-Pauline' writings. We should be careful, however, not to use that prefix with the usually dismissive connotations it has for us. All these writings, in their different ways, stand in their own right and it is important for our purpose to understand just a little of how they do so. Others might question whether this or that piece of these writings is Pauline, but we need not be detained on these questions, interesting though they remain. What we need to notice is something of the dynamic development of the biblical faith as discoverable therein. We will look at these texts briefly in turn.

Colossians and Philemon are part of one corpus and some think that the latter is genuinely Pauline. Interestingly, Colossians was written in response to a need which had arisen in the life of the Church there. Again, it was an ethical one. Concern had arisen because the spiritual practices of the Church, which were in themselves unorthodox, were giving rise to sexual immorality (Col. 2:23). The affront this caused was probably theological as much as ethical since it seemingly embraces dualistic notions of spirit and flesh which, according to the writer, were denying the supreme Lordship of Christ. The Colossian Church is seen as a salvific society into which believers have been baptised (Col. 3:3). Unseemly behaviour (Col. 3:5–9), of any kind calls this membership into question and risks invoking God's wrath. The key to salvation is, therefore, a moral one. The author goes to great pains to set out the sort of behaviour God wants between the present and the return of the Lord in glory which is still clearly expected (Col. 3:4). Love is a crowning virtue throughout (Col. 3:14), although the love commandment is not quoted as such. But here, again, it is important for us to notice, what love requires is freely worked out in the given situation with reference to every area of life and thought. It is all-pervasive and authoritative.

All this is also true of the epistle to the Ephesians, the key to which is its highly developed ecclesiology. It uses the text of the Colossians letter extensively, but, again, it uses it freely and is not bound by it in any way. Here again we see the biblical faith in the making, as succeeding generations work out its implications for themselves in their changed and changing circumstances. By the time this was written, or certainly among this community at least, the expectation of the imminence of the end had receded. It was still there (Eph. 5:16), but it is no longer the formative influence it was for so many of the other writers of the New Testament. The life of the Church is here worked out in the sort of detail required in an ongoing world. It is to be a unity founded on love (Eph. 3:17). Love is *the* ethical norm throughout and the place where its requirements are to be defined is the Church itself which was pre-ordained by God (Eph. 3:9, 11), and now called into existence for the very purpose (Eph. 1:10). Christians are to walk in the light (Eph. 5:8), and in so doing will distinguish themselves from others, share with them though they might a great deal of common wisdom about the moral life, e.g. the Household Codes (Eph. 5:21–6:9). These are also quoted in Colossians (Col. 3:18; 4:1). We will comment on this overlapping of Christian and secular practical moral wisdom in the next chapter. The introduction of these Codes so early in the post-Pauline tradition is a clear illustration of just how ready the Early Church was to innovate and develop the tradition when it saw need to do so. It must have come to see this particular need once it realised that the ongoing structures of everyday life were to remain, at least for the foreseeable future. For now, however, all we need to notice is that the moral life is here being worked out in continuity and discontinuity with the past. Neither of these dominates. Both are present throughout. Tradition and innovation go side by side.

If Colossians and Ephesians can be seen as a development of the Pauline tradition in theology and morality at one stage removed, the remaining deutero-Pauline writings can be seen as marking yet another stage. In them ecclesiastical considerations are even more to the fore. This might or might not be because they were later in date, when it was realised even more clearly that the world would be ongoing, or it could equally be that they came from areas of Church life where that was realised before it was in others. This latter is quite likely if for no other reason than this: the central paradigm-shift in the Early Church would not have taken place in the same way and at the same time everywhere in its life.

In 2 Thessalonians the author is clearly at pains to dampen expectation of the imminent end of the world, something that the first letter to them, by Paul, might have raised. Here there is no explanation of how the misapprehension has arisen. It is simply pointed out that the end cannot occur until it is preceded by certain events and that these have not happened (2 Thess. 2:1ff.). In the meantime, the good life is commended by warnings against idleness which seemed to be of a particular concern at that time (2 Thess. 3:6). The glory of the Lord Jesus is available in the here and now (2 Thess. 2:14) and every good work and word is commended (2 Thess. 2:17).

The Pastoral Epistles, 1 and 2 Timothy and Titus, are the most clearly deutero-Pauline of this group. No attempt is made here to emulate either Paul's style or vocabulary and they are usually assigned a date late in the first century or early in the second. Christians were subsequently divided over whether or not they were worthy of inclusion in the canon of scripture at all. The concerns they express are certainly those of the later Christian Church when Gnostic, Marcionite and other heresies were becoming increasingly popular. The epistles bluntly denounce these things and enjoin the necessity of faith and sound doctrine in the context of effective church organisation. By this later date the place of church officers in the hierarchy is clear. Elders and bishops, who might be the same, are to preside and adjudicate on what is and is not allowable. Rudimentary though these orders are at this stage they were clearly to become the models for what was to follow. Indeed, this very point would go a long way to explain their subsequent popularity among holders of such offices who, of course, also by virtue of them had the authority to afford these writings canonical status.

Only 1 Peter makes love at all central to the moral life (1 Pet. 1:22). For 1 Timothy it is the goal to be aspired to (1 Tim. 1:5), but it is to be qualified by other considerations (1 Tim. 6:11). For our purpose we need to notice this degree of freedom of interpretation on what was previously, albeit as we have seen in different ways, the central motif of the Christian moral life. This is an important illustration of just how quickly and freely the developing Christian Church adapted its message. It did this, as we have again seen, right from the beginning, so the popular view that there was to begin with a 'pure' faith which later became adulterated, is a quite false reading of the facts. There never was such a thing. Different writers facing different needs emphasised different things from the beginning. They did this in continuity and discontinuity with each other as they took and left whatever they wanted from each others' writings and traditions. 1 Peter is different again. It follows Colossians and Ephesians more clearly than the Pastorals do. Believers are again enjoined to be distinctive in their behaviour (1 Pet. 4:3), not because this will help them to attain salvation, but because it exemplifies the fact that they have achieved it in their own communities.

This journey through the later writings of the New Testament continues to be the subject of ongoing scholarly debate, but we have now considered enough of it for our purpose. That has been to show that the text of the New Testament throughout is one of change, adaptation and innovation and nowhere more so than in how its writers approached the moral life. Although recurrent themes, such as love, are discernible throughout, they are handled freely and differently under different circumstances by various writers who all had distinct things urgently to achieve in their care for the Churches.

In the next chapter we will extrapolate from all this some of those themes and emphases which remain perennially important for the Christian moral life. In doing so we will see that they are not the ones many Christians and non-Christians suppose to be important. We will also see they are at the centre of what it means to call any particular understanding of that life a Christian and a biblical one.

Chapter Five

THE DYNAMICS OF CHRISTIAN ETHICS

In the previous chapter we had a brief insight into the way the Bible sees the relationship of faith to ethics and how its writers worked constantly at trying to understand the moral life required of them and the ever-changing communities for which they wrote. We saw that they invariably quoted and developed what others had written and said before them, and that they also developed it for their own purposes in what became a cumulative tradition. A tradition which ended arbitrarily somewhere around the beginning of the second century CE, after which, again arbitrarily, and for reasons which had to do with the needs of the developing Christian Church at the end of that century and later, it was decided which books would be in the New Testament and which not. This was and remains for some a matter of controversy. The canon, or rule, of scripture is something defined by the Church. Initially it accepted the four Gospels and the thirteen Epistles of St Paul. By the beginning of the third century it placed these alongside the Old Testament, but the story of the formation of the New Testament canon was then far from over. Some parts of the Church accepted some other writings and other parts rejected them. The New Testament as we have it was not finally recognised until a Council in Rome decreed it authoritative in 382 CE, but even this did not end continuing controversy.

All this is a window on what we are calling in the title of this chapter a 'dynamic'. This word is deliberately used to draw attention to the fact that the biblical life in all its general diversity and, in particular, in its under-standing of morality, is one of an ongoing process in which writers focus on the needs of the moment and on the light their knowledge of God throws on them. In all this, as we have repeatedly seen, method and style is more to the fore than content, important though that remains in the background. What we have briefly looked at, is the making of the biblical faith in its ethical dimension. It was never complete at any one time in the biblical history. Something more always had to be done, in situation after situation and by succeeding writers, to bring their faith to bear on the actual circumstances of the lives of the faithful. We have already noted above that all this came to an arbitrary end, not because the task had been completed, not at all, but because the needs of the life of the Church changed as the biblical era gave way to a continuously developing Christian tradition. The biblical faith went on being made, but in a different way, outside the canon of scripture. The point here being stressed is that the seeming break between scripture and tradition is an artificial one. It arose from extra-biblical circumstances in which the Christian Church needed its own canon of scripture for political and theological reasons which had nothing to do with scripture as such.

In spite, therefore, of the seeming break between scripture and tradition which has, of course, been exacerbated by the elevation of scripture above tradition, certainly in Protestant belief and by attributing to it a difference in kind from all that was to follow, there is in reality no break at all. Roman Catholic orthodoxy has, by comparison, avoided this mistake. The biblical faith was made and remade throughout the scriptural era. It was the focus of the religious life from the earliest Old Testament beginnings right up to the latest writings in the New. It embraced both continuities and discontinuities, but it was always recognisable. This faith went on being made and remade in the Early Church. It did not stop. And, this is the point we shall now see to be all important: *it goes on being made and remade.* The biblical faith, therefore, is still in the making. And it will remain so this side of the Kingdom of God. Neither the biblical writers, we, nor any who come after us will know everything we need to know to complete the making of that faith entirely to God's satisfaction. We are not God, so the biblical faith we make will always be an aspiration. All it can hope to do, therefore, by God's grace, is the best it can, not by dint of its own efforts, but by faith and an enabling grace. We will return to this more fully in chapter 7. For now, all we need notice is that the making of our faith and the moral life which goes with it, in the midst of our own life and times, is coterminous with what we read in the Bible. It is neither different from nor secondary to it. It is one and the same. This is why it is so necessary for us to read the Bible carefully in the first place. Only when we see how others made their faith, can we realistically go on doing so for ourselves.

By the same token, we need equally to apprise ourselves of Christian tradition and the way it has made and remade the biblical faith in its ethical dimension. Again this has happened, just as it did in the Bible, in relation and response to changing times and needs. All this is part of the seamless tradition in which we stand and to which we must make our contribution if we are to be true to ourselves as the women and men of the Bible and Christian tradition were true to theirs. As well as owing this to ourselves and the integrity of our faith, we also owe it to those who will come after us as they turn back to see what they can learn just as we have done. All this is why we earlier rejected the popular post-modern assumption that our age is so different that it cannot be in a continuous relationship with the past at all. We called this an unacceptable arrogance of presentism and rejected it in favour of an understanding of life in general and the Christian life in particular which is continuous with the past. That does not mean, of course, that it is in all respects the same as what went before. It is clearly not. Just like Christians in any age we face new challenges and some of them are undoubtedly novel ones which we might well have to deal with in novel ways. But none of this means either that the past is totally alien to us, or that we can learn nothing from it to our benefit. The reverse is true for theological, and ethical as well as for pragmatic reasons. Our dilemmas and the uncertainties, which feature in seemingly all of them, may be new, but uncertainty has always been part of human life, even if we now feel its force in new and more demanding ways. We have explained this in earlier chapters and will reflect further on certain ethical issues which demonstrate more acutely the problem of uncertainty in the next chapter. Only there will we see just how the Christian ethical tradition, as we have been understanding it, is more appropriate to our situation than is commonly supposed. Appropriate, because it helps us face uncertainty not by denying that it exists, or believing that it can be countered with certainty (we have already seen in chapter 3 why this is impossible), or that we need to despair in the face of it. It is appropriate because it helps us to cope with uncertainty to the best of our ability and, ultimately as we shall see in the final chapter, by the grace of God.

We will now draw out of the last chapter the main themes and emphases of the biblical morality as we there understood it. Throughout the New Testament these themes run into and interact with each other to such an extent that separating them out is, of course, an artificial exercise, but it will at least serve the purpose of bringing them into a focus that we can use in the next chapter when we consider the contemporary application of Christian ethics to areas of modern morality in which we are uncertain. Before we do that, however, we will have to ask, in the conclusion of this chapter, some general questions about their nature and the possible manner of their use in this way. We will also consider briefly the actual relationship of morality to religion.

Relationship to True Piety

Morality and being human are related throughout the biblical traditions because they are related in the being of a righteous God. In the New Testament, as the knowledge of God became available to all so too did God's righteousness; so much a focus, as we have seen, for both Matthew and Paul. This knowledge of God required nothing less than complete righteousness. Those who claimed to have a knowledge of God but who did not practise complete righteousness, such as the Pharisees, were accused of hypocrisy. The treatment of the Pharisees in the New Testament is a complex subject and their piety and morality has, in fact, much to commend it. In its style it is not that far from that of many latter-day Christians. Its reconciliation of ideals on the one hand with practicality on the other is something we will discuss later, since the need to accomplish that reconciliation in some form or other is a perennial one. The Pharisees were not alone in being condemned in this way, since priests, Levites and others came in for similar harsh criticism in the teaching of Jesus. In that, righteousness is portrayed as being so powerful that it cannot be contained in 'systems' or 'codes' of morality. It is all-pervading and, for that reason, more likely to be practised by the outcast and sinners than by the official guardians of virtue, whoever they may be. At this point the parable of the Good Samaritan says it all (Luke 10:25–37). It is special to Luke's Gospel and, therefore, probably something which circulated later in the life of the Early Church and this might explain its absence in the other three, which made the same point in different ways. The exposition of the parable has often suffered from a common tendency to reduce the piety of the New Testament to a weak ethical point. Namely, be nice to people. There is far more to it than that. The priest and the Levite were probably no more or less nice to people than anyone else, but they had religious reasons which controlled when they could and could not be so. These were what prevented them from crossing the road. Neither the priest nor the Levite were at liberty to touch half-dead bodies, if they did they would become ritually defiled. The Samaritan had no such difficulties. His response was spontaneous, genuine and unstinting to the point of being self-sacrificial. With no thought of either piety or righteousness the Samaritan fulfilled the requirements of both and in so doing inherited eternal life. The lawyer who asked the question about this topic, to whom the parable was a reply, was enjoined to go and do likewise.

This is Luke's way of making a powerful point which is made throughout the New Testament: true piety and true morality are one and the same thing and the most common reason why it is not practised more is that piety, and not morality, is so frequently misunderstood. Its institutionalisation is its death and can only be a pale shadow of its manifestation in the spontaneous acts of unselfconscious people acting from the right motives. All this, of course, raises profound questions to which we will return later. Morality cannot exist only in what is spontaneous and unselfconscious if it is also to become part of the fabric of the societies in which we live. This is why, as we will see, there is compelling reason to believe that there are and need to be two moralities and not one. That said, however, the consistency with which the New Testament and the Bible generally stress the fact that piety and righteousness are inseparable from a way of being stands. It makes it impossible for us ever to suppose that there can be a Jewish and Christian morality without it. The aspiration to do whatever is morally right is something which affects our whole beings and our relationship with our creator. This is the heart of a religious morality properly understood. True piety and true morality are one and the same thing. This can never be otherwise in a world created by a righteous God which is peopled by God's creatures who are created in God's image.

Non-reciprocity

Although the Lord's Prayer makes it clear that Christians are to forgive because they are first forgiven by God, Jesus advocated an intrahuman ethic which is strictly unconditional and non-reciprocal (Matt. 5:46; Luke 6:32). It categorically rejects any assumption that good should be done to others with the expectation of being treated likewise. This is nothing different from the eye-for-an-eye and tooth-for-a-tooth morality. 'Even the heathens do as much' is the harsh judgement of Jesus on this as a motive for doing the right thing. This is the basis of the injunction of Jesus that we should love our enemies (Matt. 5:44) because, only in so doing, can we make it clear that our actions are not inspired by expectation of reward from those to whom they are done. By this radical means, the ethic of Jesus rejects all thought of revenge or retaliation, particularly in the name of righteousness. There can never be scapegoats who are vilified in order simply to establish the right-eousness of those who carry out the vilification. This is nothing less than a manifest failure to love our enemies, however justified we may feel when we do it, given the frequently horrific circumstances which seem to make it necessary. Righteous indignation of this kind is as sinful as the sin it is directed against, a timely reminder that our vices stem as frequently and easily from our supposed virtues as they do from our more blatantly obvious sins.

It is, of course, not unnatural that many Christians interpret all this as requiring non-resistance to evil however impractical that may be at times. In this they join cause with those who are pacifist for numerous other reasons which as Christians they might or might not share. They, therefore, are always ready to turn the other cheek even to the point of refusing to protect others when they have the opportunity to do so. Christian pacifism, as such, continues to be a radical and, in these ways, consistent response to the Gospel injunctions to love one's enemies. The lack of self-interest and, more to the point, lack of interest in the welfare of loved ones and others could not be more consistent. In the next chapter we will see why this inter-pretation of the Gospel injunction to love enemies is not so construed by (probably) the majority of Christians. The reason for this, as we shall see, is that when the New Testament is interpreted in this way it bypasses any obli-gation to place our morality in the wider context of a theory of civil society, something the Christian Church has had to do ever since the conversion of Constantine in the fourth century CE. But all this is part of a wider discussion to which we shall return frequently in what follows. For now we simply note what a radical and central part of the Gospel morality the emphasis on non-reciprocality is.

Unconditional Lengths

Matthew chapter 18, verse 21 records Peter as asking Jesus how many times a brother should be forgiven if the brother persists in sinning and Luke chapter 17, verses 3–4 parallels this in the parable of the Two Debtors. The answer, of course, is 'seventy times seven'. The point being that individual Christians do not have any authority to draw lines. Seventy times seven is unlimited. Only God has the authority to draw lines.[1] Nothing sinners can ever do and, more to the point, no matter however many times they sin, can ever, for that reason, cut them off from the forgiving grace of God as it is mediated through the person who is sinned against.

This is an often repeated theme of the parables. It witnesses to a theological claim about the relationship of good to evil which is fundamental both to the New Testament and the wider thought of the Early Church as it developed from it. Namely, that the triumph of good over evil in the ministry, death and resurrection of Jesus is complete. The most eloquent expression of this in the New Testament is, of course, Paul's great prose hymn (Rom. 8:31–39). Nothing at all can ever separate anyone, sinner or virtuous, from God's love in Christ Jesus. This central theological theme became the more important in the Early Church as it opposed Gnostic and other tendencies infiltrating Christian orthodoxy with the claim that there was an eternal dualism between good and evil in which the latter could never be finally vanquished. The injunction to forgive without limit is the implication of all this for the moral life. Any refusal to forgive is a tacit acceptance of the imperviousness of evil to goodness. Here again we see the consistency which exists between the theology and morality of the New Testament, however differently the various writers might have chosen to express them.

Anti-establishmentism

We have noticed throughout the extent to which, and the frequency with which, Jesus was at loggerheads with those around him about the nature of morality. Its mention in all the Gospel records causes it to stand out as something which we can safely assume is an authentic mark of his teaching. Jesus was, clearly, a protester. A protester against the establishment which was more used to protesting itself than being protested against. In this sense he is the anti-establishment figure *par excellence*. The fact that his name is now invariably used in so many ways to justify the establishment is an irony which should escape no one. This is made possible, of course, because those in establishment positions who so use his name often seem to suppose that their bit of the establishment is above or free from his criticism. This will clearly not do. The teaching of Jesus cannot be tamed in this way, necessary though it remains for it to be socialised and institutionalised in appropriate social, political and economic structures. We will return to this question below. For now we need to be clear about just how radical, consistent and purposeful Jesus' anti-establishmentism in morality actually was.

First of all, it was an anti-establishmentism which was exemplified in Jesus' lifestyle: the way he dressed, the company he kept, the way he questioned the most cherished of institutions such as marriage and the family, the way he ate and drank and with whom he did so and the way in which he disregarded even the most seemingly self-evident considerations of prudence. So many of his replies to questions were enigmatic to say the least, to such a degree that we cannot but conclude that they were meant not as alternative solutions in themselves, but as pointed challenges to his hearers with but one aim: that of imploring them to think again from first principles and, in so doing, to take nothing for granted. In all this, he did not seemingly proffer solutions at all, they were left to be found by those who questioned him in the first place.

He did, however, give clues as to where solutions could be found and these were equally anti-establishment, because he pointed to the spirituality and morality of the outcast and the despised. These were not those who were just outside of acceptability in the societies in which he moved; they were the actually reviled. Those for whom there was no hope whatsoever. In all this, it was affront enough for establishment figures to be themselves challenged, for them then to be compared so totally unfavourably with those they despised must have been the final insult and humiliation. Such people were despised in every way; for their beliefs or lack of them, for their manners, often for their jobs and for their morality itself. It is impossible at this point to resist the temptation of imagining what the reaction would be in our polite societies if this were to happen to them and, more to the point, to us. We would feel humiliated and discredited and be more likely to harden our attitudes than to re-examine them, to rely on reports and resolutions which are attested signed and sealed, rather than be prepared to think again. In all this we would rely, no doubt, on the sheer numerical strength and weight of the establishments to which we belong and from which we would draw solace. Perhaps it is only by musing in this way that we can begin to understand even a little of the sheer power of Jesus' anti-establishmentism. Again, we will return to this below. The next feature of Jesus' ethical teaching we will discuss follows from this one.

The Search for Novelty and Innovation

So often in what Jesus said about morality he seemed to be encouraging his hearers to try something which is not just slightly different from what they are already doing, but something which is totally different from it, so different, in fact, that it defies the imagination. New Testament writers all witness to this in their different ways, they so often seem to be reaching for solutions which are just around the corner. St Paul, in particular, exemplifies this. We have seen how he wrestled constantly with questions about what the life of faith required morally in this and that situation against the background of trying to work out what freedom from the law actually meant and how the excesses to which it so often led could be controlled. And this is also true of all the New Testament writers. Commenting on this Leslie Houlden writes, 'we can see that each writer has his own moral "world" in which he lives, his own pressures to respond to, and his own problems to solve'.[2]

There is another important point to notice in all this. Individual writers were not consciously, it seems, reflecting on the implications of what they wrote for anyone other than those they immediately addressed. We would not, of course, at all expect them to have written for the posterity they have enjoyed, but we might reasonably expect them to have had a broader consciousness than they invariably did have. They were focused on the here and now, on whatever, seemingly, was on a particular agenda in a given situation in the full knowledge that it would change again, for whatever reason. Even granted that our world is so different and that whatever we write has to be written in the awareness of what it will mean for this situation and that, we cannot but be struck by just how focused and even exclusive the New Testament writers were in their concerns about morality. We have already had frequent reason to observe that, draw on others though they freely did, they never seemed to think that this limited their own freedom of thought, expression or action in any way.

The Place of Self and Self-interest and of its Denial

We have seen that the Great Commandment in Matthew chapter 19, verse 19 and chapter 22, verse 39, which is repeated and alluded to elsewhere in the New Testament (Mark 10:17–23; Luke 18:18–24), is a quotation from Leviticus chapter 19, verse 18 and considered how central it is to both Jewish and Christian morality. It carries, however, an ambiguity which has been reflected throughout Christian history. Does it affirm self-love or does it deny it? Does it mean that we cannot love others unless we first love ourselves, or does it mean that if we do so we cannot love others? Luke, at least, is clear in his answer to this question. 'Whoever comes to me and does not hate father and mother, wife and children, brothers and sisters, yes, and even life itself, cannot be my disciple.' (14:26.)

Some have taken this to enjoin an extreme ascetic denial which is not, of course, unique to Christian morality. It has certainly not been typical of its mainstream interpretation. It might also be thought that denial of self-love enjoins martyrdom, but that is not so seemingly self-evident. Martyrs do not necessarily disregard the value of their own lives in sacrificing them. Indeed, the impact of their martyrdom is the greater if we suppose them to value their lives and yet decide to give them up. In the main, Christians have allowed for degrees of self-worth, esteem and love on the grounds that all creatures are created in God's image, including the self, and are therefore to be valued for that reason. Others, on this view, are loved because the loving person has experienced God's love in the first place. 'Love one another, just as I have loved you' (John 13:34) is, therefore, the dominant Christian motif. But poignantly even here, it is an enigma since Jesus ultimately gave his life as he did. On the whole, prudence has prevailed in Christian thought on self-love and, as a result, its place has been recognised along with the equal recognition of the dangers of its excesses. For all that, however, Christian morality places a central emphasis on *agape,* God's love for God's creatures as a love which is totally self-giving even if it is not totally denying to the point of self-denigration. This is the love that Christians are to love others with because they have first experienced it themselves. What it explicitly does not allow are any conscious considerations of self-interest when the interest of others is being contemplated and acted upon.

All this has been at the centre of an ongoing controversy in Christian tradition which has focused on the nature of the relationship between human and divine love. Human love, *eros,* seeks the self-satisfaction of desire. *Agape,* seeks only the well-being of the other and does not consider self-satisfaction at all. St Augustine sought to combine the two in *caritas,* something which is achieved when human love reaches out and is met by and freed from its limitations by divine love. For some, especially those in the Lutheran Reformed tradition, this solution of the relationship of the two loves left too much room for human love, thereby opening the door to the achievement of virtue by human rather than by divine effort. As a result, they emphasise the all-pervading nature of divine love over human, and for them human love is only the divine love in action.[3]

Mention of this ongoing controversy about the nature of Christian love has served to illustrate how understandings of the self and self-love are central to the Christian ethical life. We will need to discuss this more fully in the final chapter when we look at the place of grace in that life. For now, all we need to note is that this issue is one of the central motifs of Christian morality.

The Use of Secular Wisdom

This is important to notice because it can be so easily overlooked. We are blinded to it by our supposition that what is Christian about morality is what is revealed and, therefore, of divine rather than human origin. In later Christian tradition, again, the debate has been between what is 'natural' and what is revealed and it remains of importance as we strive, as always we must, to try to discern the relationship between the divinely created order and the revelation of the divine will.

In the New Testament when its writers were so often struggling to find out what sort of life the life of faith was to be in all its necessary detail, they frequently accepted prevailing Jewish and secular wisdom. We have already mentioned a central example of the former: the so-called Household Codes which are found in Colossians chapter 3, verse 18 to chapter 4, verse 1 and Ephesians chapter 5, verse 21 to chapter 6, verse 9. There is much scholarly debate about whether or not these codes in the New Testament contain anything really different from the seemingly identical extant codes which existed in contemporary Jewish writings and in Greek and other ancient Near Eastern cultures. The version in Ephesians does reflect on the husband–wife relationship as a mirror of the relationship of Christ to the Church, but it otherwise conforms to prevailing religious and secular wisdom about the virtues of subordinate relationships in households and similarly closed social groupings. It brings nothing really distinctive to these and, therefore, stands as a clear example of the way in which Christian morality embraced secular morality in important areas of life such as this.

Direct quotations from prevailing secular wisdom are not common in the New Testament, but the fact that they exist at all shows, at least, that there was, for many Christians at least, no objection in principle to embracing what was secular if it seemed appropriate to do so. Another much quoted example is that found in 1 Corinthians chapter 15, verse 33: 'Do not be deceived: "Bad company ruins good morals." ' This is virtually a direct quotation from Menander of Athens the fourth-century BCE dramatist who wrote that 'evil communications corrupt good manners'. Doubtless such an obvious truism would have existed in many different forms and would have been, perhaps, common in everyday speech. If so, then it is all the more confirmatory that New Testament writers and readers found quoting everyday secular wisdom quite acceptable, in principle at least. It certainly looks like an acceptable feature in Christian ethical discussion; a part of its spontaneity, whatever seemingly came to mind when its writers wanted to communicate in earnest. If this is so, then we might muse that nothing much changes! We do not, any more than the New Testament writers did, live in a world of Christian thought and action which is separate from the wider world around us. In the business of everyday living what is and what is not Christian is invariably and inevitably blurred. It has always been like this and will remain so this side of the Kingdom of God.

There is, of course, much debate about the relationship of Christianity to culture, which is what we have been briefly touching on, and I have recently written about it at some length elsewhere.[4] Suffice it for us to notice here that what is Christian and what is cultural is and always will be blurred and this is as much the case about Christian morality as it is about anything else. Noticing, as we have done, something of the way in which secular wisdom and practice overlap with Christian morality in the New Testament reminds us, again, that its world and ours are remarkably similar in this important respect.

The Ultimate and the Everyday

New Testament discussion of morality moves with seeming ease between the confidence with which it speaks of ultimate things and the provisionality with which it speaks of the mundane. The lofty requirements of God's love and righteousness go side by side with working out what they mean in relation to the everyday and the specific. One way of seeing the relationship between these two is to say that they are of a piece and that for that reason the everyday always conforms to the ultimate. This is, however, clearly not the case since no little of the time and effort of the New Testament writers is given to trying to understand the relationship of the two. And so it is, of course, for us. The New Testament writers were, no more than we are, able to be sure in each and every situation that they had said the last word. This is a timely reminder to us that, not only is the biblical faith still in the making, it always has been and always will be incomplete. This is why the making continues and it does so nowhere more clearly than when it tries to reconcile the ordinary and the everyday with the ultimate in morality.

In all these and other ways the New Testament writers were seemingly driven by a desire to solve what were everyday and contingent ethical problems; what was most problematic at any given time for the people they cared and wrote for. In doing this they did not tie up all the loose ends and what they wrote often led to further problems, as we have seen was the recurring case in what they said about divorce. All this is a far cry from what many suppose to be the case about New Testament faith and morality. It belies the truth of supposing, as many Christians do, that it contains all the answers to all ethical problems for all time. Equally, it belies the obverse view that there is an inflexible givenness to what it says that prevents it from coming to terms with modernity and novelty. Both of these views are mistaken. Pious believers are wrong in thinking that the New Testament is something it manifestly is not, and unbelievers are frequently wrong in not questioning that view in the first place. The actual truth about New Testament morality, as we have seen, is far more complex and interesting. It is also far more relevant to our ethical situation as we analysed it in the opening chapters. Its relevance lies more in its method than in its content, in the way it grapples with the pressing and the confusing, rather than in the inflexibility of what it says.

All systems of morality exist between a polarity of ultimate values, or systems, on the one hand and contingent needs on the other; between what really, ultimately matters and what can or cannot be done in given situations. The best moralities are those which are creative and flexible in the way they achieve their ends. Ones which ignore neither what is ultimate nor what is contingent. Ones which hold both of these polarities in equal regard and tension. Distortion occurs whenever this does not happen; whenever what is ultimate is used to disregard what is contingent or vice versa. Moralities which deserve to be taken seriously are those which keep both sides of this polarity in play. This is what we have seen the morality of the New and the Old Testament do *par excellence*. It roots all ethical value in the being of a righteous God who has a loving relationship with God's creatures and creation. A God who leaves them, God's creatures, to sort out what their faith and best moral endeavour requires in this situation or that.

All this is a far cry from what most Christian believers and unbelievers suppose biblical morality to be. In this chapter we have briefly highlighted some of the reasons why this is the case. We have now seen how a Christian and biblical morality has at least eight dynamics: first a distinctive relationship with true piety; second, a commitment to non-reciprocity; third, a commitment to go to unconditional lengths; fourth, a location which is anti-establishment; fifth, a capacity to seek novelty and innovation; sixth, an elaborate sense of self and the denial of self-interest; seventh, a willingness to use secular wisdom; eighth, the location of the contingent in the ultimate.

Before we apply this eightfold dynamic to particular contemporary ethical problems, it is necessary first to clarify further the relationship between metaphysics and morality. The dynamic which has been identified has not drawn heavily on Christian doctrine. The Trinity, so loved by O'Donovan and others is not prominent. The main reason for this is that we are developing a biblical morality and the Trinity in its credal form is not found in the Bible. The one seeming mention (Matt. 28:19) is generally thought to be a much later interpolation. Given that this is an important area of debate, it is necessary to make explicit the relationship between morality and metaphysics which is here being taken.

The relationship between metaphysics and morality is linked to the relationship between duty (where knowledge of a moral absolute is applied to all situations) and the situation. This subject was importantly essayed by A.D. Lindsay in a small book, *The Two Moralities,* in 1940. It is apparently not often quoted and has probably not received the attention it deserves. Lindsay calls the two moralities: that of 'my station and its duties' and that of 'challenge or grace'.[5] The former is the moral code of the society in which we happen to live as it might be interpreted in relation to whatever we do or whatever function we fulfil in society. The latter is what we feel inspired to do in any given situation; ordinary things, in which we feel the need to be innovative, creative and even surprising; to be prepared to discover something new. The two are contrasted, he claims, in a number of ways. The morality of 'challenge or grace' is: not what is always expected; it anticipates no reciprocity; it might have a certain extravagance; it is outside the sphere of claims and counter-claims; it is not concerned with this or that social structure; it considers outer actions as expression of inner life; it puts persons before 'society'; it appeals to love and imagination; it is not necessarily connected with religion.[6] We will discuss this latter part below since it is clearly central to our discussion. Before doing that, however, we first need to notice what all these features of the morality of 'challenge' or 'grace' have in common. To begin with they are untrammelled by anything. By this is meant that they are their 'own thing'; free, responsive and creative. They look neither to the past nor the future, the two sources by which moral actions are usually most constrained. They do not deny the legitimacy of the morality of duty and, indeed, may in turn have an effect on it. They do not excuse the acting moral individual from doing her or his 'own thing'. As such they may well require courage and self-sacrifice and may even attract ridicule.

The resonance between all this and the dynamic of Christian morality as we have here come to understand it will be obvious. Far from it not corresponding to that teaching, it seems to fit it entirely. This is the main point of this book; the ethical teaching of Jesus is more resonant with a morality of challenge, spontaneity and grace than it is with the rigid system of morality with which it is more generally identified. Lindsay also argues this very point and comes to the conclusion that: 'The Christian life is not the fulfilling of a prescribed code of exacting duties. It demands an attitude towards a perpetual quest, always something more to do something more to find out.'[7]

How different all this is from generally accepted views of what Christian morality is all about. Here it is something which is an activity more than it is anything else. Something to be done creatively and joyfully, rather than something carried out as a matter of formal duty. Something which encourages openness and innovation against conformity to convention. Something the excitement of which is always yet to come, just around the corner waiting and even demanding to be discovered.

It is always encouraging us to find better solutions to old problems. To do better tomorrow. Let an anecdote make the point. The late orchestral conductor Georg Solti was being interviewed, not long before he died, by a young interviewer who asked him when he had been at his best as a conductor. 'Tomorrow', he replied, shooting out of the chair. The Christian ethic wants a reaction from us which is very much like that. It is something yet to be achieved, commensurate with the about-to-be, able to make a difference to it and effect continuous innovation in the amelioration of the human lot. Something that can turn the rhetoric of morality into effective action. Something that shows us where to begin not only in morality but also in religion. This latter point will need to detain us a little in the conclusion of this chapter before, by way of example, we apply the Christian morality so redefined, to some contemporary ethical problems in the next.

No religion can have a monopoly of morality, so defined. The reason for this is that in the end it is left to individuals to decide what to do, either singly or together. Indeed, as we have repeatedly seen, religion often inhibits morality, so understood, because it stifles it with convention and propriety of one sort or another. It is too self-conscious, too considerate always of its own position and interest, too certain and, above all too judgmental. However, this does not mean that religion cannot be an aid to morality, it is but to point out that it is not always the aid it is thought or claimed to be. Lindsay, again, observes that it is incorrect to think that religion leads to morality in the sense that it can be read off from it.[8] This is an important, though not of course original, idea. Kant made the same observation in making the point that whilst morality does not depend upon religion, it, nevertheless, leads *ineluctably* to it. He also held the view that Christianity was the most moral of all the religions because it was the one which most supported the moral code. The point here is that morality needs religion and leads to it, without it, it is directionless; it has no aims, aspirations, or context within which to function. The life of faith and theology is here seen as the consequence of the moral challenge. It is the challenge which breathes life into them and not the other way around. Religion can, indeed, direct and sustain moral endeavour, as we have seen the case to be with the Christian understanding of love. Once the doctrine of rewards is removed, as we have seen it must be, as a reason for doing good, then religion provides only the means of morality. It cannot also provide the reason for it. That can only come from the unselfish will of the moral agent, out of a deep desire to do the right thing in the interests of others. Here the only well-being calculated is that of the recipient of moral action; that of the moral agent does come into it, but only in small measure, in the sense that an element of self-esteem is proper, according to the Christian view of the moral agent, because the agent is also created in the image of God and is a recipient of God's love.

All this is the exact reverse of seeing religion as having all the answers to life, including and especially moral ones, as being all-powerful for that reason and requiring abject and unquestioning obedience. As we have seen, such a religion is usually thought of as *revealing* moral truths, of making something known which cannot effectively be known in any other way, although other ways might be seen as confirming what is revealed. All this was, and still is for many, part of a two-worlds dualism in which the other world has all the answers for this one. This is untenable for the simple reason that the other worldly metaphysic on which this dualism depended is now seen to be an impossibility. As the result of applying philosophical rigours, which have been well known and widely accepted since Kant wrote his great *Critique of Pure Reason* in 1781, we now know that the sort of metaphysics on which the two-worldly view of religion, or anything else come to that, depends is untenable. We can only begin to understand morality if we start honestly from where we are and not from some incomprehensible place where we are not.

Traditional believers can be heard clearly protesting at this point. This, they claim, denies faith. By this they imply that 'faith' is the acceptance of things we cannot ordinarily know; better still, impossible things, the more impossible the greater the faith. Traditional religion and morality can be as crude as that. When it is, it tries to make a spiritual virtue out of believing the impossible and, even more disastrously for its own cause, making the acceptance of believing that its threshold. The Queen in *Alice in Wonderland* saw through the sheer nonsense of all this with memorable clarity when she pointed out that believing impossible things was so easy that she could even do it as many as six times before breakfast. The same nonsense as that of debating the number of angels on a pinhead – you can have as many as you want and, if it makes you feel the better, do have as many as you fancy. This is not true religion. The proper name for it is superstition. It would not be necessary to point all this out here so forcibly if it were not for the fact that what we are objecting to here is what the majority of Christian religious believers seem to believe. Little wonder that Christianity is so widely rejected by people who instinctively know this is nonsense, even if they could not put forward the well-known philosophical arguments for proving it to be so. All the more sad is the fact that, rather than think through their position, so-called orthodox believers become even more entrenched in their position by pointing to unbelievers and saying that the reason why they, the others, cannot see the light of religion is because they will not make the leap of faith. The leap to believing impossible things. A leap into nothing, in fact.

In direct contrast to what we have briefly seen much religious 'orthodoxy' to be, it is here suggested that religion does not require us to believe impossible things at all, certainly not as a precondition of its acceptance. What it does do is provide us with a wider context in the light of which we can do impossible things, aspire that is, to the moral life. We will discuss more exactly how religion does this in the last chapter after we have considered examples of the application of morality, so defined. Only then will we be able to see more clearly just what it is a religion like Christianity has to achieve if it is to command our respect and allegiance.

For now, all we need to be clear about is that we are understanding the moral life and the challenge it presents us all as the starting point from where religion can be discovered. The moral life is not the end of religion, it is its beginning. We can make a start at it simply by being honest with ourselves. No more than that. We need only to want to try to make some sense, from where we stand, of the beautiful, mysterious and often fright-ening world in which we find ourselves. Not for selfish reasons, not for what we will get out of it, but for what we can put into it and do so, as we will see in the last chapter, by the grace of God. In doing this we will do well to be aware that we are making common cause with all women and men of goodwill and moral earnest, whatever their religion, creed or ideology. We are setting out only to ask pressing questions about the moral life and whether or not a religion like Christianity can help us answer them.

We have already seen that 'starting from here' in this way is not new. It is, in fact, what many Christians have tried to do following Kant for the reasons we have briefly considered. In the history of modern theology this began with the writing of Frederich Schleiermacher and his *magnum opus, The Christian Faith*. In this book he based theology on the experience of dependence, rather than on philosophical arguments which Kant had already shown to be false. He based theology on what we could actually know, or experience, not on philosophical speculations, which by the time he wrote were known to be demonstrably false. Theological development at this time was intense and rapid. Two things broadly happened to it. There were those theologians for whom the strictures of Kant meant nothing. They continued to write as though the older certainties and presuppositions were still intact. They reached back to Aquinas with maintained confidence and this is continued by writers in the constant development of that tradition. Other theologians followed Schleiermacher in the realisation that theology had to start again from new beginnings. Not, of course, that it had to eschew all that went before, far from it. What it had to do was to reinterpret older traditions in the light of the new philosophical discoveries.[9]

In essence, the post-Kantian theologians were not doing anything new or particularly novel. Western theology has always developed in the light of philosophical insight. Most famously, Augustine did it in the light of Plato, and Aquinas did the same in the light of the newly discovered texts of Aristotle by medieval Islamic scholars. The technical term for this is 'apologetics', the exact description of what theologians do under these circumstances. They explain theology to those who have come to see the world in different lights. These latter are what we would now call 'paradigm shifts'. They are what happens to human understanding when changes to it are brought about by major new discoveries in the arts and now, with increasing frequency, in the sciences.

The story of 'modern', which I usually take to mean 'post-Kantian', theology is well and fully told. Kant really did bring about one of history's all-time paradigm shifts. He put the knowing subject at the beginning of all knowledge, whereas hitherto the 'objects' of knowledge had occupied that position.[10] This simply meant that philosophy was to begin again, from where we could be sure of starting without question; from human perception and experience. Hence the reaction of Schleiermacher and others who have followed him ever since.

There is no space here or particular reason to trace the story of modern theology since Kant, but it will be helpful for our purpose to notice one of its most recent developments. It will at least serve to show that this debate is still very much alive and yielding important results for those who want to understand theology in the light of Kant's momentous work. For our purpose, we need to notice how it has consequences for understanding morality which are in many ways identical to the conclusions we have already been arriving at in this chapter.

Don Cupitt is a Cambridge theologian who, now for over thirty years, has been exploring the contemporary relevance of what we have called post-Kantian theology for faith and morality. He has done this in successive books which are written in an accessible theological style and are, as a result, widely read, influential and controversial. Many who have criticised him have failed to notice that he is writing in a theological tradition which goes back to Schleiermacher and also has precedents in nineteenth-century English theology. It is important to remember this if for no other reason than to remind us that Cupitt is not the lone maverick his opponents often claim him to be. He stands in a proven and respectable theological tradition.

In one of his early books, *Christ and the Hiddenness of God*, Cupitt pointed out that 'We have come to a time when we apprehend the world, describe it, and cope with it in ways which have no connection with the concept of God.'[11] In acknowledgement of Kant, Cupitt re-explored the meaning of the Lutheran insistence that theology is better employed when it studies the nature of human salvation than when it studies the existence of God for its own sake. Here, again, is the classical post-Kantian starting point for theology: human experience. By 1980, in *Taking Leave of God,* he came to see with unmistakable clarity that, 'the old kind of religion, a thoroughly heteronomous external control-system, is gone and swept away by history'.[12] Christian religion and morality had to come to terms with human autonomy, just as secular morality had done since at least the beginning of the eighteenth century. In the ensuing popular and widespread theological debate, Cupitt's position was described as standing for theological 'non-realism'. This means that his theology was not premised on the reality of things we, in truth, have no knowledge of the reality of at all. It was premised, rather, on human experience, on what we can know and be sure of. Spirituality, what humans feel and experience, is to precede doctrine and belief of any kind. 'Religious truth', he writes, 'is practical. It has to be chosen and done, for it is a matter of the will.'[13] Historically, it is as though Cupitt had just come to his writing from listening to Kant lecture. The resonance between the two really is as strong as that and the ensuing debate about Cupitt's work would have been the better if this had been more widely acknowledged than it has been. At the very least, it would have set that debate in its proper and mature place in the development of modern theology, rather than caricaturing Cupitt as some latter-day maverick with no intellectual pedigree. Whilst everything he has written stands eloquently in its own right, it is clear to all who read it carefully, and are privileged to know anything of the disciplined way in which he has developed his thoughts, that he is the conscious and self-acknowledged heir to an accomplished tradition in modern theology. We turn now to a consideration of the implications of Cupitt's work for Christian morality. He has explored this himself in *The New Christian Ethics*.[14]

Cupitt points out that his interpretation of, what we have seen to be post-Kantian, 'anti-realism' in theology means that we can no longer construct a morality which is premised on there being objective ethical truths which exist independently of us and which are valid everywhere and for all time. 'The human condition', he writes, 'is utterly gratuitous and contingent, and there is nothing out there antecedently for us to live for or to live by.'[15] As a consequence, we have to create value by the exercise of our wills. In this way, ethical acts are acts that bring about something that has not previously existed. They are entirely voluntary in the literal sense of that word. He comes to the conclusion that: 'The morality that it is rational to prefer is the morality with the greatest power to inject value into life, and that morality is the Christian morality, which gives worth to the worthless and justifies the ungodly.'[16] This morality is redemptive in the sense that it creates value where, often, none exists and, in the very act of doing so, redeems what is fallen or lost. It is not and never will be complete and always leaves everything to be done. At least the surface resonance between all this and the view of Christian morality we have reached here will be obvious. Cupitt, however, wants a radical break with the Christian past and believes that the 'new' Christian ethics that he seeks will not be attainable without that break. The Christian self, he argues, has to be reinvented in the here and now. We have given reasons for not taking this view and for preferring an understanding of the present moral task which draws on previous, and especially biblical, experience but which is not bound by it. Indeed we have also seen why the Bible is best interpreted as itself advocating a morality of this kind. In this way, we can be inspired by the Bible without being at all bound or inhibited by it. The same is true of all subsequent Christian history, including what we might or might not have done yesterday. All that is, likewise, there to inspire us. It does not inhibit us in any way as we seek to create value in our lives in the Christian tradition and by the grace of God. We begin to touch here, of course, on major themes in contemporary theological debate and there is space only to do so in passing. It is nonetheless important for us to do so.

Recall that we saw earlier that religion does not precede morality, but that morality, rather, leads to it. It can, of course, lead to secular philosophies and ideologies either as alternatives to religion or in part. The point is that morality needs some sort of framework. It cannot exist without some such wider reference because it is a shared human activity and endeavour; one which we have repeatedly seen to be of the very essence of what it means to be human. Historically, it is the great religions of the world that have essayed this very thing and, on the whole, they have done so more enduringly than have philosophies and secular ideologies. Contrary to what some believe, there is no such thing as an inevitable process of secularisation in which religions are forever giving way to secular philosophies. Religions do change, of course, but they also endure, and they probably do so because they have created frameworks for morality.

Here the Christian religion is used as the framework for morality for reasons we have been exploring throughout and will return to in the final chapter. No special or exclusive claims are here being made for Christianity, beyond noting that it does this particular job extremely well, as we have seen Kant and Cupitt both claim in their own ways. Christianity best enables us to use it in this way if we, in fact, deliberately refrain from claiming too much for it. Not only in relation to what it can deliver (we have discussed this often), but also in relation to what it can deliver in comparison to other religions and ideologies. Morality, like everything else, now not only has to exist in a pluralist world, it can have no credibility unless it visibly does so. This means that whatever religion or ideology it might espouse, it must also be mindful of and respectful towards all women and men who are morally earnest, whatever their religion or ideology. Only in this way can particular moralities now serve the wider interests of all human beings. The old Christian exclusivist view of itself as the guardian of supreme truth and morality has to go. Just as it has to do in other religions which make similar claims. It is premised on an arrogance which the world can no longer indulge in, if people are to live together in real peace and harmony. Indeed, the acceptance of this very point is now best understood as a pre-condition of moral sincerity. It is what allows members of a religion such as Christianity to find their morally earnest place in the wider world. Not by denying or subordinating the moral integrity of others, but by seeking in proper humility to live alongside it and do with those others the very best that can be done in the interests of all. Wilfred Cantwell Smith put this extremely well when he wrote:

> The two most fundamental questions confronting twentieth-century man, the one social, the other personal, both involve religion: how to turn our nascent world society into a world community, on a group level; and on a personal level, how to find meaning in modern life.[17]

At the very least, this requires religious moralities such as the Christian one, to be earnest in their seeking of world peace and environmental integrity. Unless we can all live on this planet without killing either ourselves or it, the future for the human race is a bleak and, probably, totally futile one. This is the scale of the challenge of modern morality. The one we have to aspire to amid all its attendant uncertainties, by meeting its myriad demands, both great and small. All systems of morality should now be judged in large part on whether or not they can help us to meet this challenge. As we have seen throughout to be the case with the Christian one, this will require them to be revisionary of their own basic premises wherever necessary before they can be seen to be sincere about their pursuit of the very best interests of all human beings. The agenda all this leads to is an urgent and immense one. This is where not only Christian morality but also the very integrity of the Christian faith itself is put to the test. If it is found wanting here it will be of little or no use at all, other than in the provision of solace for any who either turn away from the world or who want to persist in believing that their faith enables them to live with false illusions about certainty. These illusions are, in truth, part of and not the solution to the moral problems we must urgently address.[18]

In the next chapter we turn to discussion of examples of Christian ethicality, as we have understood it, at work. Whilst they are chosen almost at random from an endless list, they will nevertheless show how seemingly intractable ethical problems which are permeated with uncertainty yield to Christian morality as we have understood it.

Chapter Six

SEX, DRUGS AND WAR

We have now seen, in some detail, why Christian morality is far from the staid thing it is usually mistaken for. On the contrary, it is innovative, challenging and above all, open-ended. It encourages us always to see things in a new light, particularly one which is different from that shed by received wisdom and tradition. It also lays upon us the immense burden of thinking very carefully before we make up our minds to do anything morally. With this and all the things we identified in the previous chapter in mind, we will now, so to speak, put Christian morality to the test by looking at some contemporary ethical problems which are the cause of widespread concern. We will only consider examples briefly and from the point of view of our subject matter, since thorough consideration of any single one of them would take more space than is here available. It is important, however, that we look at more than one such example, so that we can get the general feel of what it is actually like to do Christian ethics in the creative way we are suggesting it needs to be done. The thing which, by now, will have become immediately obvious to us is that the Christian approach to morality positively encourages us to be innovative to the point of changing our minds about received wisdom and formerly accepted solutions. In a way, there is nothing particularly novel about this. Christian morality has always been changing and evolving and, in doing so, has sometimes been through what can only be described as quite major changes. They have, perhaps, been seen as less dramatic than they are because they have taken so long to come about. For example, the traditional Christian acceptance of slavery as a social institution was not overturned until the horrors of modern slavery became widely known in the early nineteenth century. The Act abolishing it in British possessions was not passed until 1807 and since then the anti-slavery movement has become widespread as a matter of fundamental human rights. We take all this so much for granted and know the history so well, that we are in danger of overlooking what a massive shift of Christian opinion this actually was. The world, moreover, has now changed so much that such shifts of opinion will, naturally, take place much more quickly. Often so quickly that we have cause to be concerned about the pace of change itself, quite apart from anything else.

One example of a recent and, by comparison, quick change of Christian ethical opinion concerns the liberation of women brought about by the feminist movements. Christianity, as we must now fully recognise, was unwittingly compliant in preserving notions of male supremacy and domination in Western culture. Indeed, it undoubtedly played a major role in this to such an extent that some commentators think that it is incapable of being reformed on the issue.[1] For the most part, however, the need for reform has been widely recognised and rapid processes of change have come about. Two of the most notable have been the Christian recognition of the harm done by the use of sexist language, particularly in Christian liturgies, and the exclusion of women from the formal Christian ministries and from representation in other professions in at least proportionally acceptable levels. As a result, even quite recent Christian liturgies are being willingly rewritten and the ordination of women is more widespread than anyone could have imagined, say, only fifty years ago.

These two changes of ethical opinion are nothing less than dramatic and fundamental and it is interesting to observe how the first took eighteen centuries and the second has effectively come about in half a one. We must expect this acceleration to continue and now be prepared to live through similar changes of ethical opinion which will take place, seemingly and by comparison, overnight. Indeed, most people will now have to live with the fact that many such changes may well take place within a single lifetime. For example, again, only twenty-five or so years ago, it was widely presumed that cohabiting couples would not normally be married in churches and unfavourable comment could be expected if they were. Today, such cohabition is a widely practised and accepted fact, to such an extent that hardly anyone would be married in a Christian church, in the UK at least, otherwise. Not, of course, that there is anything particularly new about this or, for that matter, about couples seeking marriage only after they have conceived. The latter was a widespread and accepted practice in rural England as even a brief cross-reference between any parish's Marriage and Baptism registers will reveal. All this was part of a rural way of life in which the family unit was central to the well-being of every member of it, particularly the elderly for whom there was, effectively, no other provision. This might serve as a timely reminder that the things which often cause us uncertainty are not always so novel as we might think at first sight. It can hardly be disputed, however, that the present pace of change is generally and consistently more rapid than anything that has gone before. Little wonder that all this inculcates, amongst other things, the sort of uncertainties we considered in the first two chapters.

Yet another major change is currently taking place in Christian morality and we will consider it at a little more length. It concerns human sexuality in general and homosexuality in particular. We will discuss the latter first. In Christian circles and society generally, homophobia is common and it acts as a visible barrier to the acceptance of change. A widespread belief in the fact that Christianity prohibits sexually active homosexual relationships does much to reinforce this. We will discuss this below. Such homophobia is a mixture of fear, prejudice and often sheer ignorance. It consolidates people into groups and creates distances between them and often makes those on both sides incapable of communication with each other. In spite of all this, however, and to their credit, many of the Christian churches are now insisting on the full and thorough discussion of the subject and, as a result, are in the vanguard of developing public opinion. The controversy this often causes invariably receives inordinate media and other attention, but that does not detract from the ongoing persistence with which the churches are, for the most part, approaching the subject. Central to the discussion is the now increasingly widespread recognition that an individual's sexual orientation might not be a matter of free choice and may well be and remain ambiguous. To that end, the churches have done much to bring about the recognition of homosexuality as a part of human experience which has to be understood as something which is for the most part a given. Something which is as it is and which, for whatever reason, we cannot change. There are those, of course, including Christians, who disagree with this. For them sexual orientation does remain a matter of free choice and they go to inordinate lengths, often in the name of evangelism, to get people who are homosexual to change their minds, lives and practices. The homosexual disposition is, however, increasingly looked upon as something which most individuals are not themselves responsible for and about which, therefore, ethical judgements should not be made. So far so good, on the way to a much healthier society than those in which homophobia dominates.

The problems which remain, however, largely concern the specific question about whether or not the degree of acceptance so established can include the further acceptance of homosexual cohabitation and erotic homosexual genital activity. The House of Bishops of the Church of England published in 1991 a statement entitled *Issues in Human Sexuality* and it has been the subject of lively debate ever since. Whilst this report called on the Church to 'listen to its homophile brothers and sisters and for [it] to deepen and extend that listening, finding out through joint prayer and reflection a truer understanding of that love that casts out fear',[2] the statement, nevertheless, concluded that Christians must still believe that all sexual relations outside marriage are sinful and that 'homosexual practice [is] especially dishonourable'.[3] The discrepancy between this comment and widespread actual acceptance of heterosexual cohabitation is, of course, obvious. The Church, therefore, called for all homosexual people to be abstinent and went out of its way to point out that clergy could not enter into sexually active homophile relationships because of 'the distinctive nature of their calling'.[4] The General Synod of the Church of England debated the Report in July 1997 and committed the Church to an ongoing educational process which was to focus on listening and toleration from all parties. This is very much the situation in the Church of England at the present time. It has also committed itself to work ecumenically on the issue with other churches in the UK and elsewhere who find themselves in similar positions. In the meantime, the issue clearly remains unresolved.

The biblical views on homosexual relationships all refer to individual instances and show no awareness of the modern conception of homosexuality as an orientation, natural or otherwise. Whilst the House of Bishops' report took the view that the Bible enjoins abstinence from same-sex sexual activity, that view is not unchallenged. There are, in fact, very few references to it in the Bible. A central one in the book of Genesis chapter 19 seems to attribute the destruction of Sodom and Gomorrah to homosexual acts, but it is more likely that the object of condemnation is the homosexual rape of divine messengers. The condemnation of homosexual acts as such has to be read into the text at this point and the same is arguably true of the other biblical references (Lev. 18:22, 20: 1–3; Rom. 1:26–27; 1 Cor. 6:9–10; 1Tim. 1:9–10). The one in Romans, for example, is more clearly directed against homosexual lust in connection with the main topic of discussion at that point, which is idolatry. Here again there is need for more careful discussion and reading of these texts than the Bishops' Report acknowledges. As we would expect to find, following our earlier examination of biblical morality, the Bible does not take a view of the issue at all and the few places where it does mention the subject all occur in the context of the discussion of other things with which the concerns of the writers are noticeably more marked. Jesus, of course, is never recorded as mentioning the subject. Clearly, the Bible does not give us an answer to the problem at all, any more than it does on other such specific issues. We have to think things out for ourselves.

We can begin to do this by recognising that the very willingness to enter into discussion on the part of so many churches is a good thing to do in its own right, providing that it is a genuine and active discussion. It may well take a long time for anything to come out of this process, but we should be patient in the confidence that that will happen. Meanwhile, however, the problem will not go away and many homosexual Christians are left to suffer from confused messages about their situation and what they can or cannot do about it. Among these are to be found devout priests and ministers with accomplished ministries. Many of these were ordained in different times when blind eyes were often turned on what was long considered a private matter. Real and commendably open discussions are taking place, but there remains widespread suspicion, opinionating and distrust. Something more must be done; but what?

We might begin by recognising that this debate is not just about private sexual activity at all and that it is a distortion of a deeper underlying issue to pretend that it is so, important though that activity remains. It is also a debate about lifestyle. What triggers many people's homophobia is the way some homosexuals blatantly display their sexuality for whatever reason, perhaps as a protest against their experience of alienation from heterosexual society. Whilst the need for that protest is a dire one about which something needs to be done, and whilst those who resort to it need our understanding and sympathy, it often brings out the worst in people on both sides of the argument.

Two important other factors have to be remembered at this point of the debate. First, there is always an inevitable and welcome discrepancy between the official view on such matters as it is represented in Church documents and resolutions of their Synods and the accepted views of significant numbers of their members among whom views vary tremendously. Moreover, bishops and others who ordain clergy often do so in the tacit knowledge that those they are ordaining are homosexual, practising or otherwise. None of this is done irresponsibly. On the contrary, this is clearly one of those 'problems' which are better resolved through careful management and sensitive patience by all concerned. Much is achieved in this way, far away from confrontational headlines, and understanding is thereby deepened on all sides. This is where real progress is already happening and from where solutions to the problem will emerge as official positions come to terms with what is practically and successfully the case. The present situation concerning the remarriage of divorcees in the Church of England, illustrates this well. The General Synod of that church has not yet approved such remarriage, in spite of producing two excellent reports over twenty years ago making it clear that there is no theological reason why it should not do so.[5] In the meantime, clergy have addressed the urgent and pressing pastoral needs of those seeking such remarriage, by quietly getting on with it according to the law of the land. In this they are encouraged by all but the most pedantic of bishops. The result is that there now exists in that church an accepted discrepancy between the official and the actual positions on this pastorally sensitive matter.

The point is that all this is unlikely to change overnight. There will always be differences between what churches hold officially and what they do in practice, and there will always be widely varying differences in those practices within their ranks. Indeed, those churches which are perhaps most successful in all this know these things very well and yet strive to hold people together. None of this should be lamented. It should not only be accepted for what it is, it should be looked upon positively as a profound response to the human needs which are generated by these and other such ethical problems. These debates about the meaning and purpose of human sexuality will continue to be of central importance to human well-being. It is salutary, perhaps, to remember that it was not until 1930 that the Church of England Lambeth Conference recognised at all that sexual activity had a role to play in human relationships beyond procreation. Again, the pace of change is rapid, speaking historically, and it will increase. In these and other ways, the churches are finding themselves at the centre of a great debate about human sexuality. Because it has ramifications for the whole of society, they are doing that society a great service in sustaining the debate as they are doing and must continue to do. It will never be resolved in the sense that final solutions will be found. All that the churches and others can do is to find ever new ways of understanding the mysteries of homosexuality and human sexuality in the hope that they will lead to the betterment of the human lot.

Another area of human sexuality which requires sustained debate and action is prostitution. The dynamic and innovative essence of Christian morality can perhaps be encapsulated by the call for its decriminalisation.[6] In what briefly follows we will see that there is much to commend this.

As the often repeated joke reminds us, prostitution is as old as human existence. People, mostly men, have always paid in one way or another for sexual favours in relationships which are arranged solely for the purposes of gratification. It was an accepted fact in many ancient cultures and even a part of some religious cultic practices. The call for its suppression among Christian groups did not become at all strong until the Reformation, by which time the fear of the spread of venereal diseases in Northern Europe was becoming a matter of widespread concern. Attempts to bring this control about, however, have been notoriously ineffective. It is, as such, not illegal in the UK and elsewhere, although it is so, seemingly without much apparent effect, in the majority of American states. What is illegal in the UK is soliciting for the purposes of prostitution and this has the effect of driving prostitution underground as though it were, in fact, itself illegal. It is, therefore, put in the hands of criminals who not only organise the soliciting, but also, invariably manage the women who, for the most part, provide the services. The result of all this is that prostitution is a widespread human activity which thrives particularly in the anonymity of towns and cities everywhere and is very largely managed by criminals of one sort and another. Since most of these are also involved in drug dealing, the two activities invariably become inseparable. Women and others who provide the services for prostitution are, therefore, managed by people who are accountable to no one and interested only in financial gain from what they do. The consequences of all this are too well known to need setting out in anything other than passing mention: human exploitation on a massive scale, the risks of disease, and the social destruction of cities and elsewhere. And all this in our very midst and we, seemingly, want to do nothing about it, or at the very least, are always quick to find reasons why we cannot do anything in spite of our protestations. For the most part, we neither question our disapproval nor think at all seriously about how to manage the phenomenon of prostitution beyond leaving it to criminals to do so on our behalf. Something is wrong in all this, very wrong.

The degree to which, as we have seen, Christian morality demands self-examination clearly points to the fact that in the face of such a problem we should begin by examining our own attitudes towards it. They are almost universally marked by self-righteousness. We disapprove of prostitution so vehemently that it never occurs to us that, in so doing, we are actually, and in large part, thereby exacerbating the problem. Not, of course, causing it to come into existence, but to exist in the unsatisfactory way it does.

Clearly, something innovative needs to be done and, for the reasons we have discussed, the Christian faith is as good a place to look for that as any. We can well begin by dropping our righteous indignation about the evils of prostitution. We could then go on to understand the phenomenon and talk rationally about what can or cannot be done about it. If some of the activities on which prostitution immediately depends for its very existence were decriminalised, society would be free to take responsibility for the phenomenon instead of handing that responsibility over to others out of a sense of misplaced righteous indignation. As long as we fail to do this we will continue to be part of the problem we are complaining about. Recall how often Jesus pointed that out to his hearers who earnestly enquired about righteousness, only to be told to put their own house in order first of all. Our houses are no more immune to the need to do this than were those of the people who so often came in for Jesus' criticisms. So often when we read the text of the New Testament, we see how the criticisms apply to others, without it even occurring to us that we are equally guilty and to blame in our own ways.

So, what would follow from all this? First, we should have concern for the welfare of prostitutes themselves. They should have access to fairness and not be economically exploited as a result of their own vulnerability as they now so commonly are. Their health should be protected and monitored; their children looked after. They should have access to counsellors at all times, so that they have every assistance in giving up what they do, if that is their wish. Drug counselling should be available. Every effort should be made to provide alternative employment for them. In this way society would be on their side. It need not at all condone what they do to achieve any of this. Although some might argue that there are far greater evils in the world than two people, for whatever reason, freely deciding to have sexual relations in this way. Indeed, some manifestly greater evils, such as child abuse and rape, might even be mitigated thereby.

None of this, of course, solves all the problems, but it does clearly proffer better solutions and general prospects than those presently available. One other obvious problem is *where* could such de-criminalised prostitution take place? Indeed, the cheap jibe 'would you like it in your street?' is often heard at this point. Of course not, but some would rather that, than what we have at the present time. Industrial and semi-industrial areas which are not used at night would, for example, be an obvious place to look for a solution to this aspect of the problem. One such could and must be found. Best-practice elsewhere should be carefully studied. Until and unless we are prepared to get involved in some such ways then things will not change for the better and the problem will get worse. Never was the Christian capability to be innovative, imaginative and unselfregarding in morality more needed than it clearly is in this tragic area of human activity and suffering.

Above all, these debates in the churches about sexuality should be maintained and kept in proportion. In this the mainstream churches have more to their credit than is often recognised. They do keep up an ongoing dialogue with such contemporary ethical problems, individually as well as collectively, through the institutions of the ecumenical movement and in particular the World Council of Churches. Indeed, in achieving all this, the churches must at least be recognised and appreciated for holding and sustaining such debates in a changing world and in this, they perhaps achieve more to their credit than most. Our society is in the throes of great debates about human sexuality and they are here to stay. They are complicated, of course, by ever new phenomena such as the now worldwide AIDS epidemic and these rightly call for even more changes of attitude and practice, particularly in under-developed countries.[6] The dynamic nature of Christian biblical morality is not only well suited to cope with all this, it is far better suited than many other ethical systems. It does face the facts, does have the courage to be innovative and, above all, is able to remain open-minded.

We will now consider another area of modern life which requires similar widespread debate. Again, we will see that because Christian morality, as we have defined it, is as it is, it is particularly well-placed to contribute to this. It concerns the ever-increasing phenomenon of proscribed drug-taking in all its forms. There is, of course, nothing new about this. Human beings have always ingested for pleasure substances that are harmful to them and they will continue to do so. In the West, alcohol and tobacco have been the most widely used for this purpose and society has long adjusted to coping with them. Whilst they are both increasingly socially controlled, particularly smoking tobacco, neither is illegal. Indeed the attempt to make the consumption of alcohol so in the United States of America in the 1930s led to social disaster and general debacle. The levels of success (and failure) governments have generally been able to achieve in the regulation of alcohol and tobacco are premised, for the most part, on not making it illegal either to possess, consume or trade in either. They therefore become socially and economically acceptable, particularly the latter because their very popularity make them ideal vehicles for sustained indirect systems of taxation.

Throughout the world most mood-modifying substances, 'drugs', are made illegal in one way another and a concerted international effort is in place to control the sources of supply, given that the points of delivery are so notoriously difficult to monitor. These substances range from the so-called 'soft drugs', which are the least physically and psychologically harmful to the 'hard drugs' which are extremely so if taken for prolonged periods. Among these are the so-called 'designer drugs' which are marketed for specific recreational purposes. The extent to which such drugs are taken in particular places is not actually known, but all the indications are that it is not only more widespread than is generally believed, it is also everywhere on the increase.

The parallels here between our general reaction to all this and to the phenomenon of prostitution could not be clearer. We equally, and equally righteously (that is the point), disapprove and the consequences are identical; we hand the whole thing over to the criminal and the unscrupulous to manage on our behalf. The social consequences of this are, again, identical. Not only is human suffering caused on a massive scale, the phenomenon is unbelievably socially destructive. Just one illustration of how it is so will make this clear. Drugs cost a lot of money to purchase from dealers, who are often dealing mainly for the purpose of sustaining their own intakes. The sums involved are dictated by market forces of supply and demand, rather than by the actual value of the substances transacted and they are, for that reason, inordinately high. Few who take drugs on any scale can sustain the sort of lifestyle necessary to earn the money to purchase them in the first place. The result of all this is obvious: resort to criminality, prostitution (again), theft and burglary. It is generally estimated, for example, that currently some 70% of burglaries in the UK are drug-related. The general situation, moreover, is manifestly out of any sort of effective social control and it is steadily getting worse. Here, again, something dramatic is called for. Not just a 'well we could try this' approach. Something different. Again, the parallel with prostitution is obvious.

We should begin by contemplating the possibility of decriminalising drugs. Again, the righteous will protest: 'it will not work', 'look at Holland' (whatever that actually proves). Of course there will be problems if this is done. That is not the point. The question is: will they be greater or lesser than the problems we have at the moment? We do not, of course, have all the answers to that question, but we must at least be prepared to ask it in the first place. Unless we do we will never know.

But will that not, the righteous can be heard to protest yet again, encourage the problem? But what precisely is the problem? Are all these substances equally injurious? And are some of them more so than alcohol or tobacco? It is not true that everyone who takes cocaine, for example, ends up either being addicted to it or progressing to 'harder' stuff. Of our righteousness, we might like to think that, but we are deluding and justifying ourselves if we do. It is manifestly not the case, and we should think again. This is a clear example of an ethical problem which we have to approach with rigorous empirical honesty and fidelity. Suppose, for the present, that we do find some substances to be comparatively harmless, should we then not think about making them legally available at much lower prices than those at which the illegal market supplies them? And could we not, in so doing, bring the whole thing effectively more into the open, where proper care and, again, counselling could take place? Why do we not even begin to entertain such an approach? Largely because, again, of our righteous indignation. The same strictures apply against this as should always apply. We must put that righteousness aside and begin afresh. As we do so we will not, of course, find all the answers immediately, but we might begin to ask new questions which will perhaps enable us to find some of them.

If we begin in this way, we might discover other things to our surprise and thereby be able to ask yet more innovative questions. Take an extreme one. Why not legalise all drugs, 'hard' as well as 'soft'? Do not those who are seriously addicted need our care and attention even more than those not so? Could we not do more for them if we brought them out of the shadowy underworlds they are constrained to live in, into a world where they would be cared for and not exploited? One in which they would not have resort to criminality to feed their addictions; a world in which they would find every help to cure themselves rather than every incentive not to do so, which is what is being encouraged by those who miserably benefit from their condition? We should at the very least begin to ask these questions with manifestly more open minds than we are currently and seemingly prepared to do.

Here again, the ethical resources of the Christian tradition, as we have understood them, can be a great help to us. They enjoin us to be non-judgmental, to have the courage to want to do something effective about an area of manifest human suffering, to sustain us as we do so and enable us to join with others who want to leave no possibility of making progress with this problem unexamined. Here again, the excitement and challenge of the Christian moral life comes to the fore and it is quite the reverse of what it is so often mistakenly thought to be. None of this answers every question and doubt we might have. Nor does it pre-empt the incredibly hard work which is needed to achieve anything. What it does is to encourage new ways of looking at things in order that we might find new solutions to the problem.

A good example of such a new solution in the UK at the moment is the initiative being taken by the British and Irish Governments, and others, to find new solutions to the problems in Northern Ireland. (Though, even as I write, these tentative solutions are in a fragile condition and might fail.) What had previously happened there was that, with every good intention, successive Secretaries of State had, in effect, talked down to the problem in the sense that they were seemingly more ready to prescribe solutions to it than listen to why these were not acceptable. In this way, without perhaps realising it, they reinforced old prejudices and positions. The new thinking, which began with initiatives by John Major when he was Prime Minister, talked up to the problem by listening and being prepared to think and do things which were previously thought to be impossible. The Secretary of State brought an instinctive flair to all this and carried things rapidly forward. Such innovative and, creative thinking echoes the Christian approach we have outlined. That is not enough, of course, to guarantee its success in any given instance, we have to take responsibility for that ourselves, but the resonance between the styles of approach is clear and that alone should give encouragement to all. Once again, we are bringing to the fore a religious ethic which is dynamic, innovative and, above all, exciting. Before discussing its distinctively religious nature in the final chapter, we will first consider just one more example of its relevance. It well illustrates all the things we have been bringing out and is an extremely important one for human well-being generally. It is that of war and peace.

It is quite possible that the earliest Christians were for the most part pacifists, although we cannot be sure either if this was so or, if it was, why. It might, for example, have had as much to do with their aversion to swearing Roman oaths of allegiance as it did with their aversion to killing as such. What we can be sure about, however, is that after the conversion to Christianity of the Emperor Constantine in 321 CE, Christians not only took up arms in greater numbers, they were forced to think carefully about the circumstances and manner in which they could, or could not, do so. This exercised the greatest minds of the day, including, and centrally St Augustine. He drew on older Jewish and Roman notions of just and unjust wars and articulated, effectively for the first time, a Christian theory of the just War. What he actually said need not detain us here in detail since record of it is readily available elsewhere. What we need to notice immediately is that Augustine demonstrated that Christian ethics is about new beginnings. It is also about drawing on secular sources if necessary, as well as it is about coming to terms with situations without preconceived set notions. This has happened to the Just War tradition ever since. In the Middle Ages it developed to take into account new sorts of deadly weapons and later it developed again to take into account the need to stop princes waging private battles. This development continues. In the face of confrontations between Iraq or Serbia and the international community, pressing questions are being asked about what the tradition means by saying, as it does, that resort to war must be a 'last resort'. And so it goes on; facing the facts on the one hand and drawing on and developing tradition on the other.

There can scarcely be a more important area of ethical concern than this. The Christian ethic enables us to grapple with it realistically and, above all, creatively. If resort to arms is an inevitability, for whatever reason, in a fallen world, then it must be disciplined and subject to the rule of law. Here again, a religious ethic such as the Christian one enables us to strive for all this, as it also helps us to strive for the creation of a better and more just world where its peoples live together in peace.

The Christian understanding of peace focuses on the person of Jesus in contrast with the understanding of peace in the Old Testament. There it was something which would happen in the future messianic kingdom (Micah 4:1–4). Until then the absence of peace and presence of war was an accepted fact of life. Indeed, war was even seen as an instrument used by Yahweh to express wrath and disfavour. All the New Testament writers recognise in their various ways that Jesus changed all that. One of his gifts to his disciples was the gift of peace and he enjoined them to be peacemakers (John 14:27). In these ways Jesus was seen as the Messiah who had brought the peace of the Kingdom to bear in a fallen world through his person and work. We have already seen, in passing, how this worked itself out in the life of the Early Church and what a dramatic difference the conversion of Constantine to Christianity made to that. All this makes Christianity a religion of peace in the sense that peacemaking is a central spiritual obligation.

This alone means that Christianity has to address itself to the causes of war as well as to the regrettable necessity to resort to it in controlled ways. These causes are, of course, legion: territorial, ethnic, ideological, political, economic and so on. There is seemingly no limit to the reasons why people will fight each other to the death. It is, therefore, necessary for Christianity to pay attention to them all, if its obligation to make peace is to be fulfilled.

Never was all this more urgent or relevant to the human condition. It is often generally observed that human beings have killed more of their own kind in the twentieth century than in all the previous centuries put together. Regardless of whether or not this could be verified and, of course, it could not, it is an arresting fact as a possible order of magnitude. It has much to do, of course, with the horrendous and varied means of destruction which are now at human disposal. Try though we must and do to keep these under some sort of control, the task is seemingly a near impossible one. We now live in a heavily armed world, whether we would wish that so or not, and news and pictures of human death, suffering and extreme distress are part of our daily diet. All this is a far cry from the belief that because human life was evolving so successfully it would not any longer need to make recourse to war, or from the belief that there could ever be a war to end all wars. It is now imperative that we do everything we can to prevent wars from occurring in the first place, and find out how to conduct and stop them when they do.

Concern about all this is something sensitive human beings should all share with each other. As they do so they bring their own religions, views of life and ideologies to bear upon the problem. We have seen that there is much in the Christian tradition to bring to bear in this way. Notice, yet again, that what is so brought is dynamic rather than static, capable of being brought to bear alongside other insights and, above all, open, adaptable and ever responsive to new needs, even unprecedented ones. This latter point is important. Because Christian morality is as open and responsive as it is, there can never occur problems it cannot face. No evil can ever overwhelm it. This is the reason for its incredible resilience and willingness to respond to new problems.

At the beginning of this chapter we considered reasons why the now incredible pace of change in the way we deal with questions of morality is affecting Christianity. The same is obviously true of all other religions and systems of morality. What we have argued here is that the ones that are now most helpful to us, like the Christian one, are those which can adapt to and help us cope with all this. Not by countering uncertainty with certainty; we considered the good reasons for rejecting that interpretation of Christian morality in chapter 3. What we have since seen is that the biblical faith and its inextricable morality are always 'in the making', and thereby ever ready to respond innovatively when the need arises.

None of these brief considerations of specific contemporary ethical problems should be read as offering solutions to them as such. They have not primarily been put forward for that purpose at all. All the discussion of them has been designed to show is that thinking radically about solutions to ethical problems which are widely thought to be intractable is not only commensurate with Christian morality; that morality actually demands that we do so.

We now turn, in the final chapter, to a consideration of the wider spiritual, religious and theological context of Christian morality as we have now come to understand it. We have, of course, already touched on this throughout, but in conclusion we need to bring it together so that we understand why the Christian moral life is like it is. We also need to have some understanding of why it is called Christian and how it is actually sustained day-in, day-out. After introductory considerations, we will focus on the relevance of the Christian doctrine of grace to Christian morality.

Chapter Seven

THE ETHICS OF GRACE

We have now come to understand the nature of Christian morality quite differently from the way in which it is commonly, and we have also seen, mistakenly, understood. In short, we have seen it to be creative, dynamic and innovative, rather than static, unchanging and inflexible. This change of view is a dramatic one. It represents the Christian ethic in a totally different light. One, that is, in which old ways of seeing problems are abandoned because new ones have a comparative ability to throw more light on them. That does not mean, as we have made clear, that what we are advocating is totally discontinuous with anything that has gone before. Quite the reverse. This new approach to Christian morality has been based on recent re-examinations of Jewish and Christian morality and, in particular, on re-examination of the place of morality in the teaching of Jesus, as well as in the New Testament generally. As a result of this, the old view of Christian morality which was premised on certainties of one sort or another has been shown to be a misrepresentation, something which does not follow consistently from the roots of Christianity at all. It is something which came into and remains in being for other reasons, the chief of which, as we have seen, is the widespread desire people have to possess certainty in their morality.

We have hardly had space to consider the psychology of those who seek certainty in morality in anything but passing references, but we have noticed throughout that moral decisions are so all-consuming of human effort and desire that people naturally want, if nothing more than out of a sense of general decency, to be sure that in any given instance they have done the right thing. More than that, perhaps, they also want to be sure that they are guiltless in what they have done and that they are not, therefore, responsible for any states-of-affairs which might, or might not, result from their actions. The desire for such certainty is, as we have seen generally, an all too human one. We saw in chapter 3 that in the Christian tradition this has been achieved either by finding certainty in the Bible and/or in the tradition of the Church. This then becomes the stuff of endless sermons in more than one sense of that word. Certainty is believed to exist, where, in fact, none exists at all. It is, bluntly, a vanity. Even worse, those who are certain in this way invariably interpret questioning as itself an act of disbelief. We have commented throughout on the incredulity of Christian orthodoxy when it is interpreted in this way. Sadly, it is doubtful if the Christian churches will change significantly in this respect. The greater the extent to which our lives are confronted by uncertainty, the more ready, it seems, the Churches are to take advantage of this by proffering certainty. All this accounts in large part for the current fashion of conservatism in Christianity and religion generally.

We have shown why no such certainty can be found either in the Bible or in Christian tradition. After that, we set about a sort of 'working distillation' of Christian morality and in the last chapter, we put it to the test in a discussion of some contemporary ethical problems. There we saw why there are prima-facie reasons to believe that Christian morality, as we have come to redefine it, is able to approach those problems in a dynamic and creative way. At this stage, there was space only to achieve this by way of illustration and pointer. We did not, in fact, solve any of these problems. That will take much more hard work and patience. All we were able to do was to show how problems which are seemingly intractable, will yield to this new approach, in principle. But success in all these endeavours out of the Christian tradition will take something much more than this, without which they will be doomed to failure. We now turn to a discussion of what it means to say that all this leads to what we might call 'the ethics of grace'. Here again we will turn back again to the roots of Christianity.

The essence of the Judeo-Christian tradition, as we have recently argued elsewhere, can be found in the ever-renewing ways in which it addresses the human condition generally and its pastoral needs in particular.[1] Indeed, 'the pastoral' is of its very essence. All the biblical narratives, in their variety and diversity, are best understood by first setting them in the context of the perceived human needs they were addressing. Sometimes they are overt in the narratives and sometimes they are covert, but they are always there to be discovered if we look carefully enough. The same is true of all the major developments in Christian tradition. Time after time, the churches are responding to new pastoral needs and adapting their thinking, and often practice, in order to meet them. In these biblical and other ways 'the pastoral' is always the catalyst for change, development and innovation. For now, all we need deduce from this is that in the Judeo-Christian tradition human need is constantly addressed.

Judaism and Christianity alike have always held that there is something seriously wrong with the human condition. The two writers of the Genesis creation narratives both held, though in different ways, that human beings now live in a different state from the one they were originally created for. It is a state of exclusion from Paradise, as a punishment for their own hubris; for thinking, that is, that they could be like God their creator. Christians followed in all this. They held the same view: that things as they now are are not as God intended them to be. Central to this is the vexing problem of the existence of evil. How can it be, it is asked, that evil of such unimaginable proportions exists in a world that was created by a loving God? Christianity does not contain an answer to this profound question in spite of the impression that it often gives to the contrary. Further, the 'explanations' it has given have themselves varied. Irenaeus, a Christian writer of the second century CE, held that the world was created by God as it now is from the very beginning so that it could be a 'vale of soulmaking' in which imperfect creatures could grow in perfection towards their creator in a life of constant recapitulation for their sins. St Augustine in the fourth century CE held otherwise. He took the older biblical view that the world was originally created perfectly but that the sin of humans had corrupted it. These two interpretations of why the world is as it is still exist side by side in Christian thinking about evil and suffering.

Sadly, all thinking people now need to ponder the problem of evil and its manifestation in human death and suffering as never before. Contrary to what was thought in the nineteenth century and up to the time of the First World War, the world, we now know, is not getting progressively better as a consequence of evolution. If anything it is getting worse. The availability of the horrendous means of mass destruction and the extent of the worldwide arms-trade explain how this has happened, but not why it has. If this does not change and change substantially, then human beings will destroy themselves sooner rather than later.

For this reason alone, the Christian doctrine of sin has never been more relevant to the human condition. It not only addresses the actual nature of the human condition, it also articulates it. In brief, it identifies the greatest sin to be the sin of pride. This takes many forms and central to them all is a belief in human self-sufficiency, intellectually, psychologically and physically. The essence of this sin lies in the human belief that salvation from the distorted human condition can be of human origin alone. Marx put it memorably when he claimed generally that whatever human beings had made they could change. In only blaming the bourgeoisie, however, Marx was blind to the fact that the proletarian masses were no less guilty. Were that it were true that human beings could change anything. The reverse is the case; so many of the things human beings make, their artefacts, get out of their control and they cannot unmake them, desire though they might that they could. Such pride affects all human activities. None are untainted. Religion, which is so often thought to be a pride-free-zone of human activity is, in fact, more prone to it than most. Reinhold Niebuhr wrote memorably of this in his Gifford Lectures of 1939, and they remain one of the greatest of all twentieth-century essays on the human condition. Following a discussion of moral pride he writes,

> The ultimate sin is the religious sin of making the self-deification implied in moral pride explicit. This is done when our partial standards and relative attainments are explicitly related to the unconditioned good, and claim divine sanction. For this reason religion is not simply, as is generally supposed, an inherently virtuous human quest for God. It is merely the final battle-ground between God and man's self-esteem. In that battle even the most pious practices may be instruments of human pride.[2]

We saw in chapter 3 and have noted above how certainty is so often sought in religion where none in fact exists. It is salutary to interpret that in the light of Niebuhr's insight.

Christianity centrally teaches that the only solution to the sin of pride that is available to human beings is, in the first instance, their own repentance for the part they play, by dint of their natures, in the world's evils. The writer of St Mark's Gospel opens his account of the ministry of Jesus with him exhorting his hearers to 'repent and believe in the gospel' (Mark 1:15). All of the other gospel writers similarly portray Jesus in this way. This requires a total turning from what is human to what is of God as a matter of mind, action and will, an unconditional seeking for forgiveness and a new beginning. This is the foundation of all Christianity, piety and wisdom. There is no other. It is open, of course, to the obvious charge of being too negative about all that is human and this has preoccupied Christian thinkers through the centuries from earliest times. Pelagius, a British monk of the fourth century, argued that human beings did have the ability to do good and that in doing so they could take the first steps towards their salvation. This view can be found in the New Testament in the Epistle of James, and Martin Luther, who held the view that humans could not do this at all, called it 'a right strawy epistle'. This debate, not unnaturally, continues and, important though it is, it is not possible for us to explore it here beyond this mention. We will take the view that the repentance Christianity calls for in no way debases human nature. On the contrary, it ennobles it, by opening the way for God to do God's work in the world. The clearest way of understanding this is to see human nature as being co-creative with the divine nature. As a result, all that humans achieve is achieved by God's *grace* which is nothing other than God's work in the world, the activity of God's presence.

The word 'grace' is a translation of *charis*, the Greek word for God's gift of Godself to humankind. It is the word used in the Greek version of the Old Testament to translate God's gift of Godself in the covenant relationship God has with God's chosen people. The New Testament writers in their different ways see this as leading to a new life of faith after repentance. It is the possession of something. Something which humans receive on only one condition, that they repent of their sins. The notion is particularly prominent in Luke's Gospel where it is used to signify the message of salvation (e.g. Luke 4:2). In the Acts of the Apostles it is used to characterise the spirit-filled person, such as Stephen (Acts 6:8). For St Paul, *charis* is centrally important. It denotes the event of salvation, what happens to the believer on hearing the word of the Gospel. It includes a sense of freedom and liberation (Rom. 3:24). This comes in the person of Jesus (e.g. Rom. 5:21) and is to be understood as the tangible difference which is made by the divine presence in human life and affairs. For Paul, this is the basis of the 'new life' which is made available in Christ, what he calls a 'new creation' (Gal. 6:15). The theologian and biblical scholar Rudolph Bultmann influentially described the grace of God's presence in Christ as an 'event', something which tangibly and historically happened in a person at a specific time under Pontius Pilate. He writes:

> The grace of God, as his judicial act of grace, can…be precisely defined: It is not a mode of dealing which God has decided henceforth to adopt, but is *a single deed* which takes effect for everyone who recognises it as such and acknowledges it (in faith) – 'grace' is *God's eschatological deed.*[3]

Bultmann famously stressed that faith experience comprised grace *and* event. It was what happened to believers individually and collectively in the earliest Christian communities. Seen in this way, grace is love in action, the tangible evidence of God's presence. It unifies human beings with each other and with God. The New Testament is full of metaphors for this. For the Johannine writer it is the bread of life (7:37–39), and St Paul calls it an 'aroma' (2 Cor 2:15), and so on. It is what later Christian tradition called 'sanctification' and later still 'personal holiness'.

St Augustine, again, in opposition to Pelagius, stressed that such grace was in the first instance 'prevenient' in the sense that it pervaded human sinfulness and was, therefore, in no way impeded by it. Following repentance and faith, Augustine also held, there was a further manifestation of divine grace which renewed and reconstituted the human will, thereby enabling it to become a vehicle for divine action in a fallen world. He also calls it God's 'second gift' after the gift of life itself.[4] The Protestant reformers followed him in this. For Luther, grace was what gave faith its strength in the face of temptation. Faith, so to speak, in action. Calvin called this 'general' or 'common' grace and argued that it was abroad in the world generally and what made all human achievement possible.

From even these brief remarks it is possible to get a clear sense of the importance of grace in the New Testament and Christian tradition. Its detailed history cannot detain us here beyond concluding that it remains as central to that tradition as it has ever been through the work, for example, of twentieth-century writers such as Karl Barth and Karl Rahner. In what follows we will outline an understanding of grace which is appropriate to morality.

First, we need to be clear about the sense in which grace is an activity. It is, of course, a human activity in the sense that it is exercised by humans alone by dint of their ability to choose right from wrong and then implement the consequences of so choosing. It is an unconditional power for the good and, therefore, as such, not of human origin alone since human beings are incapable of producing such a thing because of the fallenness of their natures. Such activity is the manifestation of the power of God's love for God's creatures at work in the world.

Cannot human beings, we might then ask, do anything good by virtue of their own nature? This question implies another. Is not the view of human nature here being taken an unduly pessimistic one? Surely human beings possess some goodness, even if only that evidenced by their very existence. This view is of ancient origin. It comes from Greek philosophy which held that goodness and existence were equated. Therefore, the argument runs, a totally evil being cannot exist and a totally good one cannot not do so. This is why Origen, in the second century, taught that the Devil was capable of being saved, because from the fact that she or he existed we can deduce that she or he is not totally evil. It is also why St Anselm argued in the twelfth century that God cannot not exist because he is the most perfect being imaginable; the so-called ontological argument for God's existence which for some is still an important one.

Even this brief mention of the way the related notions of goodness and existence have been in interplay in the history of Christian doctrine shows how important it has been and remains.

The difficulty with attributing to human beings any sense of their own moral worth is, as we have seen, their propensity to the sin of pride. Instead of thinking, therefore, that they can do some good of their own natures and then having to distinguish and quantify it, is it not far the better to say that this is not possible at all? To say, that is, that they were not created for this purpose, but that they were created to serve their creator in the ways we have outlined. We might, therefore, prefer to argue that human beings exist because they have the potential for good but that, because the world is as it is, they do not have the equal power to actualise it. That power is a gift, a second gift, God's grace, which comes from the same source as the first one, life itself.

It is important to note that, for all this, we can never distinguish precisely in our actions what is of ourselves and what is of God. This can only be done from God's viewpoint, which we can never possess. Everything we think and do will, therefore, always be a mixture of the human and the divine. At the very least, however, we can be confident that God created us in a way that makes this possible.

Importantly, the visibility of that is not obliterated by human sinfulness, marred though it remains. Helmut Thielicke put this memorably when he said that humans possess an 'alien dignity', meaning by that that the divine presence is always discernible in all human life and affairs, however marred they might be by human sinfulness.[5] The redemption of all that is human, therefore, will always and even at its most complete, be an admixture of the human and the divine. It need be no less complete or effective because from the human standpoint we cannot see it clearly.

Another question arises from this and is even more difficult to answer: how can we ever know that what we are doing is of the will of God and not of our own will? Part of the answer to this must, again, be to recognise immediately that we can never be sure of this. Since we are not God we can never know either God or the mind of God completely. This will be challenged, of course, by all those who believe, for whatever reason, that this is not the case and that we can indeed both know God as God is in Godself as well as know, for certain, what God wants us to do. We have rejected this position throughout on the grounds that neither the Bible nor the Church can give us access to this sort of knowledge. We can no longer live as though we have access to the realities in, so to speak, another world, a world which will settle all our questions in this one. The only reality we know is the reality we derive from our sense-experiences of the world in which we live. That is it. All else is conjecture. This applies to all human beings whatever their religion or ideology. All are bounded by and limited to what sense-experience can make known. All the metaphysical arguments which have been hitherto used to prove otherwise are so much sophistry. They do not work. This was, as we have seen in passing, the essential message of Kant's philosophy. However, we have also argued, as he did, that morality leads to religion. It does so because it demands the ultimate of us, pushes us to our limits and denies us certainty when we reach them. The answer to this problem is, again, one which originates in Kantian philosophy.

Kant held that ideas which purport to constitute reality itself are not valid. We can have no knowledge of things-in-themselves, but we can use principles which 'regulate' our lives and conduct. He called these 'regulative ideals'.[6] They serve to guide our thought and conduct and they do this sufficiently, regardless of the fact that we do not possess the ability to turn them into metaphysical certainties. The knowledge we have of them is sufficient for its purpose, that of guiding thought and conduct. We should not ask more of them than this, this is, for all practical purposes, all that we need. To ask anything more is unnecessary because it serves no practical purpose. As long as the regulative ideals that we live by fit the facts as we perceive them, then we cannot or need not ask more than this. In the end, it is not necessary to ask anything more of the religion or ideology that we live by. Its sufficiency is to be found in the purpose it serves.

The philosophical name for this view, of course, is 'pragmatism' and it provides us with one of the only three classical philosophical theories of truth. The first, the correspondence theory of truth, claims that the statement 'X' is true if some state of affairs corresponds through sense experience to 'X'. This is what is meant by the correspondence or 'verificationist' theory of truth. It does not work in religion, of course, because we have no access to the sense experiences which could possibly verify metaphysical truth claims, notwithstanding the profundities of mystical experiences. The second classical theory of truth is the coherence one. It holds that 'X' is true if the statement coheres with all other relevant statements we might make. Much religious truth claims to be of this kind, but it too falls prey to difficulties. Our experiences of the world are so varied and contradictory that reconciling them all in coherent propositions is also an impossibility. Both of these theories of truth and their appropriateness to questions of religious truth have been widely discussed.[7] Each has its defenders. The correspondence theory is, perhaps, the most commonly held to be religiously appropriate in the sense that, for example, God's actual existence is what is thought to correspond to statements about belief in God. But this has the obvious disadvantage of making an article of unverifiable belief an article of faith.[8] That leaves the pragmatic theory of truth which we are favouring. We will now see why it affords the best possible, in the sense of available, account of what we are doing when we understand our ethical choices and actions to be acts of grace.

Pragmatism, as a modern philosophical theory in its own right, flourished first in America in the late nineteenth and early twentieth centuries. It is associated with the names of three philosophers: C.S. Peirce, J. Dewey and William James. After noting the thoughts of the first we will concentrate on the third, James. They all wrote under the direct and indirect influence of Kant. Peirce held that all thought was precursory to action and that there could be no intelligible distinction in thought which did not lead to some difference in action. Beliefs of all kinds, therefore, must be understood as rules for action. They are not worth quibbling over if the actions they lead to are the same. He cited the disputes over transubstantiation between Catholics and Protestants as an example of this. If the effects were the same, as they are, there is no need to dispute the finer points of the knowledge which gives rise to them. Peirce acknowledged that the idea of God could be entertained in this pragmatic way if it led to improvements in mind and conduct which were analogous to those anyone would derive from the company and example of another good and influential person. William James took up and developed Peirce's ideas as well as he did those of British empirical philosophers.

James's magisterial work, which is an all-time classic of its kind, is *The Varieties of Religious Experience*, first published in 1902.[9] He was an empirical psychologist who assembled a mass of detail on the actual nature of religious experiences which he recognised as being valid in their own right. He treated them as part of the world of sense-experience just like any other. They were not, nor do they need to be, in a class of their own to make sense; they made that in their own right. James wrote in a flowing and easily accessible style which had an eye for a memorable phrase. One such was his claim that all ideas should be judged according to their 'cash value', what could be done with them. Like Peirce, he also argued that there could be no meaningful distinction in an idea which did not make some difference when it was 'cashed' out.

James concluded from his empirical studies that all the religious experiences he observed, notwithstanding their varieties, had one thing in common; they all possessed something extra. The word he chooses to depict this is 'saintliness'. Of this he writes:

> The collective name for the ripe fruits of religion is Saintliness. The saintly character is the character for whom spiritual emotions are the habitual centre of personal energy; and there is a certain composite photograph of universal saintliness, the same in all religions, of which the features can easily be traced.[10]

He summarises these features as: being in a higher life than the mundane one, of experiencing the harmony between the two, of experiencing freedom as a result, and of feeling positive rather than negative towards difficulties. In summary of this, he writes, 'Religious rapture, moral enthusiasm, ontological wonder, cosmic emotion, are all unifying states of mind, in which the sand and grit of the selfhood incline to disappear, and tenderness to rule.'[11] This authoritative summation of what the religious life is like is as good an illustration of the point we are making as any. It shows how the human–divine interaction actually occurs as a common feature across the spectrum of the religious life in all religions. But how do we know if it is true or false, how do we know it appropriates reality rather than illusion? This is where James, after Peirce and others, pressed home his pragmatic theory of truth. This is contained in *The Varieties of Religious Experience*, and we will see how below, but his major systematic philosophical work on the subject was not published until four years later in 1906. It is entitled, simply, *Pragmatism*.[12]

Pragmatism is defined as a method; 'the method of settling metaphysical disputes which might otherwise be interminable'.[13] It asks, quite simply, what difference (again) 'would it practically make to anyone if this notion rather than that notion were true'?[14] It is amazing, he adds, how many philosophical disputes collapse into meaninglessness once they are subjected to this simple test, and claims that there is nothing new in it since it was employed by both Socrates and Aristotle and more recently by Locke

Berkeley and Hume.[15] It holds that '*True ideas are those that we can assimilate, validate, corroborate and verify. False ideas are those that we can not.*' (His italics.)[16] Like beliefs they are, therefore, made true or false by events. Do these events signify success or failure? Do they, in a word, work, or not? Belief in God is no different in this respect from any other. Of this he writes:

> On pragmatic principles, if the hypothesis of God works satisfactorily in the widest sense of the word, it is true. Now whatever its residual difficulties may be, experience shows that it certainly does work, and the problem is to build it out and determine it so that it will combine satisfactorily with all other working truths.[17]

In *The Varieties*, James claims that this is not only what philosophers have always meant by truth, it is also what is commonly meant by it.[18] He adds that this is the deeper way of evaluating religious truth when compared to approaching it from the point of view of endless and inconclusive metaphysical speculation. It is now time to draw out the implication of James's views, which are here endorsed, for our purpose; that of understanding ethics as 'the ethics of grace'.

A further key to the ethics of grace is that of the flourishing of human existence. Whatever is good for human existence therefore, is whatever contributes most visibly and verifiably in sense-experience to their well-being. Since we now know more than we have ever done about the dependence humans have on their fragile environment, this well-being must extend to that as well. There can be no such thing as a state of human well-being which is dependent on the exploitation of the natural order. Nor can human well-being now mean anything other than total human well-being. We live in a closely interdependent and vulnerable world in which ascendancies of interests which work against the interests of all cannot be permitted. This is why, as we have argued earlier, interpretations of religion which serve that end, however covertly, have to be eschewed. They can no longer be defended by claims to uniqueness, or any other amount of pious platitude. Their strength and perennial value will only remain if they focus on what they have in common, rather than on what they do not. The purpose they must serve is that of securing a total human well-being which is not premised on people of various religions and ideologies converting others to their point of view as a pre-condition of anything. This point has been often repeated because it is so centrally important to everything we are seeking in the ethics of grace. No one religion, let alone interpretation of a religion, has a monopoly of that, however dear it may be to us individually or collectively.

Of course, it may be objected that, although religion might function in a humanely fulfilling way, it does not always do so and at its worst it can be the opiate for human well-being that Marx and others have accused it of being. Religions have always been, are and sadly probably always will be, used as vehicles for social repression and economic exploitation. The, so-called, 'liberation theologies' of the late twentieth century have grown out of a heightened awareness of this as well as a desire to do something about it. They have not, note, abandoned religion for this purpose; they have re-constituted it by focusing on meeting the specifics of human need in this situation or that. Their success has been notable and they are good examples of how theology and religion should respond in the face of human need.

The work of grace, so understood, is the work of restoring to all human beings the divine image which is part of their natures, but which is marred by their own sinfulness for the reasons why, and in the ways which we have briefly considered. It is a wider work than we have here been discussing. It embraces 'the pastoral' in the widest senses. Morality is only a part of this, although it is an extremely important one. It includes all acts of tenderness, compassion and understanding between all human beings whatever their circumstances might be. This is because, in the Christian understanding of the relationship of humans to their creator, the human–human encounter is part of the human–divine one. It applies no less to human beings in their complex social, political and economic rela-tions, than it does between them individually. This is why there is a need for 'social theology'. It is also the reason why there can be no area of life, thought or action which lies beyond the proper concerns of the religious life, so understood. Christianity is particularly clear on this point. It holds that, in Christ, the word of God has become incarnate in all life. This restores the right relationship of creatures and creation to the creator. Other religions contain other ways of reconciling the world as it is with what they believe it ought to be and this, in all, is a large part of what they have to offer together to a fallen world, or one which is not as it was meant, for whatever reason, to be. These passing remarks are necessary only so that we are clear about that fact that the work of grace is not confined to morality alone. It pervades *all* human life, the aesthetic no less than the ethical, and the sensory no less than the rational. Its place in morality is the better understood for this reminder, if for no other reason than that we see morality as the integrated and inseparable thing it is from all other aspects of life and thought.

As rational creatures we find ourselves in a fascinating, strange, delightful and, at the same time, often frightening world. We cannot but do everything to make whatever sense of it we can. This is why, as we saw in the earlier chapters, we have no choice but to live at the frontiers of our knowledge and ability. No acts of grace excuse us from this. They can never be a total substitute for what is human, redeem human effort though they do in the ways we have seen. This means that all art and science and human understanding of every kind is part of the proper study of human beings and, again for reasons we have briefly seen, also a part of the human–divine encounter. In seeking moral integrity, therefore, there can be no substitute for hard work, not even the substitute of God's grace. That comes to our aid only after we have fulfilled all our human obligations to our creator. Serious empirical study is at the heart of all this. It is what enables us, at all times, to ascertain what is actually the case about anything, as distinct from what we might like, for whatever reason, to think to be the case. This is what makes the serious moral life an interdisciplinary one. A part, that is, of all the very best of human endeavour and discovery.

We have seen repeatedly that the moral life is part of the essence of human life itself and that its understanding is part of the understanding of that life. This is why morality cannot be exercised *in vacuo.* It has to have a framework. We have also seen why it is now widely recognised that that framework cannot only be a rational one, important though rationality is, as our immediately previous remarks have reminded us. Morality requires of us nothing less than total human understanding and we have explored why, from the point of view of Christianity and of other religions, that must include an understanding of the human–divine encounter. In these ways it relates to our comprehension of our present condition in all its manifest diversity, as well as relating to whatever we believe to be the goal and purpose of human existence. It is here that religious moralities, such as the Christian one, are at their strongest. They keep this aim in sight at all times. We have also seen that they should be judged true or false on the basis of the perceived effectiveness with which they do this. On, that is, what they are able to achieve amid the confusions of the world in which we live. The Christian life is, as we have again seen, particularly rigorous, resourceful and innovative at this point. Its truth should be judged more by how effective it is in this way, rather than by whether or not its claims to certainty are verifiable in other ways.

So understood, the moral life is inseparable from the religious life, not because religion brings certainty to it, but because it sustains us in the absence of it. More than this, even, it gives us the hope that every adversity can be overcome by the grace of God once we realise that all human effort is part of that grace, and that grace can never be a total substitute for it. It is here that prayer and worship are of central importance. It is through the spiritual disciplines, however we might understand them in all their diversity and variety, that we are able to sustain the religious disposition which, as we have seen, from a Christian point of view, is subsequent to the desire to live a moral life. Such a desire, in the end, is as good a reason for being religious as any.

NOTES

Introduction

1. Aristotle, *Ethics*, trans. J.A.K. Thomson (London: Penguin, 1955), pp. 27–28.
2. Nicholas Peter Harvey, *The Morals of Jesus* (London: Darton, Longman and Todd, 1991).
3. Ibid., p. 35.
4. Ibid., p. 24.
5. J. Fletcher, *Situation Ethics* (London: SCM, 1966).

Chapter 1

1. See R. Niebuhr, *Moral Man and Immoral Society* (New York: Scribners, 1932).
2. See W.D. Hudson, *Modern Moral Philosophy*, 2nd edn (London: Macmillan, 1983) for references to the views here mentioned. Many of the following references to theories of morality can be further studied in W.D. Hudson, ed., *New Studies in Ethics*, Vols I & II (London: Macmillan, 1974).
3. Charles Birch and Ronald Preston, *Facts and Fables in Ecology and the Integrity of Creation* (Liverpool: Hope Press, 1998).
4. I. Kant, *Groundwork of the Metaphysic of Morals*, trans. H.J. Paton (New York: Harper Torchbooks, 1964).
5. See K. Ward, *The Development of Kant's View of Ethics* (Oxford: Blackwell, 1972).
6. Ibid., p. 61.
7. Cicero, *De Republica*, III, xii, 33.

8. A.P. D'Entreves, *Natural Law* (London: Hutchinson, 1951), p. 7.

9. *On Human Life* (London: Burnes Oates, 1968).

10. J. Bentham, *An Introduction to the Principles of Morals and Legislation* (Oxford: Clarendon Press, 1789).

11. S. Kavka, 'Some Social Benefits of Uncertainty', *Midwest Studies In Philosophy*, Vol. 15, pp. 311–326.

Chapter 2

1. K. Galbraith, *The Age of Uncertainty* (London: Book Club Associates, 1977).

2. K. Marx and F. Engels, *The Communist Manifesto* (London: Penguin, 1967).

3. J.S. Mill, *Utilitarianism* Everyman No.482 (London: Dent and Son, 1964).

4. A. Macintyre, *After Virtue* (London: Duckworth, 1981), pp. 49–59.

5. D. Hume, *An Enquiry Concerning Human Understanding*, ed. L.A. Selby-Bigge (Oxford: Clarendon, 1902), p. 21.

6. Ibid., p. 25.

7. Ibid.

8. Ibid., p. 28.

9. Ibid., p. 32.

10. *Treatise* (III, I, 1).

11. *Treatise* (III, I, 2).

12. *An Enquiry*, p. 231.

13. Ibid., p. 225.

14. I. Kant, *The Critique of Pure Reason,* trans. N.K. Smith (London: Macmillan, 1964), p. 607.

15. Ibid., p. 55.

16. Ibid., p. 22.

17. Ibid., p. 23.

18. Nicholas Boyle, *Who Are We Now?* (Edinburgh: T.&T. Clark, 1998), pp. 69–93.

Chapter 3

1. See H. Zahrnt, *The Question of God* (London: Collins, 1969), p. 16.

2. Quoted by R. B. Hays, *The Moral Vision of the New Testament* (San Fransisco: Harper, 1996), p. 226.

3. Ibid.

4. Ibid., p. 238.

5. Ibid., p. 239.

6. Ibid., p. xi.

7. Ibid., p. 188.

8. Ibid., p. 204.
9. Ibid., p. 469.
10. Ibid., p. 364.
11. Ibid., p. 310.
12. Ibid., p. 294.
13. Ibid., p. 296.
14. Ibid., p. 344.
15. Ibid., p. 401.
16. S. Hauerwas, *Sanctify Them in the Truth* (Edinburgh: T.&T. Clark, 1968), p. 19.
17. Ibid., p. 32.
18. S. Hauerwas, *A Community of Character* (Notre Dame: Notre Dame Press, 1981), p. 73.
19. E. Norman, *Christianity and World Order*, (Oxford: OUP, 1979), p. 3.
20. Robin Gill, *A Textbook of Christian Ethics*, new revised edition (Edinburgh: T.&T. Clarke, 1995), p. 339.
21. Ibid., p. 341.
22. Ibid., p. 345.
23. O. Cullman, *The Christology of the New Testament* (London: SCM, 1959), p. 6.
24. O. O'Donovan, *Resurrection and Moral Order* (Leicester: IVP, 1986), p. 76.
25. Ibid., p. 77.
26. Ibid., p. 81.
27. Ibid., p. 13.
28. Ibid., p. 155.
29. Ibid., p. 183.
30. Ibid., p. 197.
31. Ibid., p. 262.
32. Ibid., p. 70.
33. *The Encyclicals of John Paul II*, ed. J. Michael Miller (Huntingdon, in: Our Sunday Visitor, 1996), p. 701.
34. Ibid., 32.2
35. *The Documents of Vatican II*, ed. W.M. Abbott (London: Geoffrey Chapman, 1966), p. 232.
36. Ibid., p. 698.
37. *Encyclicals,* p. 702.
38. *Documents,* pp. 668–669.
39. *Encyclicals,* p. 701.
40. Ibid., p. 705.
41. Ibid.
42. Ibid.
43. Ibid., p. 752.
44. Ibid., p. 751.

45. Ibid., p. 758.
46. Ibid., p. 761.
47. Ibid., p. 762.
48. Ibid., pp. 763–764.
49. Ibid., p. 765.
50. Ibid.
51. Ibid.

Chapter 4

1. See J. Pelican, *Jesus Through the Centuries* (New Haven: Yale University Press, 1985), pp. 186–187.
2. See John M. Court, *Reading the New Testament* (London: Routledge, 1997).
3. Amos 5:21–24.
4. John Barton, *Ethics and The Old Testament* (London: SCM, 1998), p. 5.
5. Gerhard Von Rad, *Old Testament Theology* (Edinburgh: Oliver & Boyd, 1962), p. 420.
6. R. Bultmann, *Theology of the New Testament, Vol. II* (London: SCM, 1958), p. 82.
7. Ibid., p. 111.
8. Hays, p. 200.
9. G. Bornkamm, *Jesus of Nazareth* (London: Hodder and Stoughton, 1960), p. 26.
10. J.D. Crossan, *The Historical Jesus* (Edinburgh: T.&T. Clark, 1993).
11. G. Ludemann, *The Great Deception* (London: SCM, 1998), p. xi.
12. Ibid., p. 14.
13. R.J. Elford, 'The Use of a Parable in Pastoral Care', *Contact*, 74, 1982, pp. 2–6.
14. Crossan, p. 417.
15. Ibid., p. xxviii.
16. Ibid., p. xxxiv.
17. Ibid., p. 421.
18. Ibid.
19. Ibid., p. 422.
20. See C.M. Tuckett, *The Messianic Secret* (Philadelphia: Fortress Press, 1983).
21. C.H. Dodd, *The Founder of Christianity* (London: Collins, 1971).
22. C.K. Barrett, *Freedom and Obligation* (London: SPCK, 1985), p. 17.
23. J.T. Sanders, *Paul and Palestinian Judaism* (London and Philadelphia, 1977), p. 47.
24. Ibid., pp. 502–508.

25. J.L. Houlden, *Ethics and the New Testament* (London: Mowbrays, 1973), p. 64.
26. Hays, p. 18.
27. Sanders, p. 51.

Chapter 5

1. J. Fenton, *Saint Matthew* (Harmondsworth: Penguin, 1963), p. 299.
2. J.L. Houlden, *Connections* (London: SCM, 1986), p. 165.
3. See A. Nygren, *Agape and Eros* (London: SPCK, 1953).
4. R. John Elford, *The Pastoral Nature of Theology* (London: Cassell, 1999), pp. 83–89.
5. A.D. Lindsay, *The Two Moralities* (London: Eyre and Spottiswode, 1940), p. 8.
6. Ibid., pp. 43–52.
7. Ibid., p. 61.
8. Ibid., p. 17.
9. See H.R. Mackintosh, *Types of Modern Theology* (London: Nisbett, 1937).
10. Kant, *The Critique of Pure Reason*, p. 22.
11. D. Cupitt, *Christ and the Hiddenness of God* (London: Lutterworth, 1971), p. 15.
12. D. Cupitt, *Taking Leave of God* (London: SCM, 1980), p. xi.
13. Ibid., p. 130.
14. D. Cupitt, *The New Christian Ethics* (London: SCM, 1985).
15. Ibid., p. 13.
16. Ibid.
17. W. Cantwell Smith, *The Meaning and End of Religion* (London: SPCK, 1978), p. 8.
18. For a discussion of the relevance of Christian morality, as generally here understood, to a range of issues see R.H. Preston, *The Future of Christian Ethics* (London: SCM, 1987).

Chapter 6

1. See D. Hampson, *Theology and Feminism* (Oxford: Blackwell, 1990), pp. 50ff.
2. *Issues in Human Sexuality* (London: Church House Publishing, 1991), p. 48.
3. Ibid., p. 18.
4. Ibid., p. 54.
5. *Putting Asunder* (London: SPCK, 1966); *Marriage, Divorce and the Church* (London: SPCK, 1971).
6. See Kevin T. Kelly, *New Directions in Sexual Ethics* (London: Geoffrey Chapman, 1998) for an excellent discussion.

Chapter 7

1. R. John Elford, *The Pastoral Nature of Theology* (London: Cassell, 1999).
2. Reinhold Niebuhr, *The Nature and Destiny of Man, Vol. I* (London: Nisbet, 1941), p. 213.
3. R. Bultmann, *Theology of the New Testament, Vol. I* (London: SCM, 1952), p. 289.
4. Edward Yarnold, *The Second Gift* (Great Britain: St Paul, 1974), p. 24.
5. H. Thielicke, *The Ethics of Sex* (London: James Clark, 1964), p. 26.
6. Kant, *The Critique of Pure Reason*, pp. 210–11.
7. See William A. Christian, *Meaning and Truth in Religion* (Princeton, 1964).
8. See, Ian S. Markham, *Truth and the Reality of God* (Edinburgh, 1998).
9. W. James, *The Varieties of Religious Experience* (Cambridge MA: T&T Clark, 1902).
10. Ibid., p. 271.
11. Ibid., p. 279.
12. W. James, *Pragmatism* (London: Longman, 1907).
13. Ibid., p. 45.
14. Ibid.
15. Ibid., p. 50.
16. Ibid., p. 210.
17. Ibid., p. 299.
18. Ibid., p. 518.

INDEX